PENG

Cooking with
VERJUICE

Maggie Beer operated the Barossa Valley's famous Pheasant Farm restaurant with her husband, Colin, for fifteen years. Since closing the restaurant in 1993, she has established an export kitchen in Tanunda to develop and make products for domestic and international markets. These include the popular Pheasant Farm pâté, their quince, cabernet, blood plum and fig pastes, the indispensable verjuice and an ever-increasing range of regional specialties.

While Maggie enjoyed her years of writing food columns for *The Australian* and other food magazines, she now spends every ounce of her energy researching and developing the new products that keep customers intrigued. Visitors to the Barossa can sample these wares and other local product at Maggie's thriving Farm Shop near Nuriootpa. Recent developments include a non-alcoholic champagne, 'Sour Grapes', which is proving successful in international markets, and exotic ice-creams such as quince-and-roasted almond, and burnt fig-and-caramel.

Maggie is the author of three successful cookbooks, *Maggie's Farm*, *Maggie's Orchard* and *Cooking with Verjuice*, and co-author of the bestselling *Stephanie Alexander & Maggie Beer's Tuscan Cookbook*.

ALSO BY MAGGIE BEER

Maggie's Farm

Maggie's Orchard

Stephanie Alexander & Maggie Beer's
Tuscan Cookbook (co-author)

Maggie's Table

MAGGIE BEER

Cooking with
VERJUICE

PENGUIN BOOKS

PENGUIN BOOKS

Published by the Penguin Group
Penguin Group (Australia)
250 Camberwell Road, Camberwell, Victoria 3124, Australia
(a division of Pearson Australia Group Pty Ltd)
Penguin Group (USA) Inc.
375 Hudson Street, New York, New York 10014, USA
Penguin Group (Canada)
90 Eglinton Avenue East, Suite 700, Toronto, ON M4P 2Y3, Canada
(a division of Pearson Penguin Canada Inc.)
Penguin Books Ltd
80 Strand, London WC2R 0RL, England
Penguin Ireland
25 St Stephen's Green, Dublin 2, Ireland
(a division of Penguin Books Ltd)
Penguin Books India Pvt Ltd
11, Community Centre, Panchsheel Park, New Delhi – 110 017, India
Penguin Group (NZ)
Cnr Airborne and Rosedale Roads, Albany, Auckland, New Zealand
(a division of Pearson New Zealand Ltd)
Penguin Books (South Africa) (Pty) Ltd
24 Sturdee Avenue, Rosebank, Johannesburg 2196, South Africa

Penguin Books Ltd, Registered Offices: 80 Strand, London, WC2R 0RL, England

First published by Penguin Books Australia Ltd 2001
This revised edition published by Penguin Books Australia Ltd 2003

12 11 10 9 8 7 6 5

Copyright © Maggie Beer 2001, 2003

Designed by Nikki Townsend © Penguin Group (Australia)
Main cover photograph by Lynette Zeeng
Other cover photography by Simon Griffiths
Illustrations by Dean Gorissen
Typeset in 10/15 pt Sabon by Post Pre-press Group, Brisbane, Queensland
Made and printed in Australia by McPherson's Printing Group, Maryborough, Victoria

National Library of Australia
Cataloguing-in-Publication data:

Beer, Maggie.
    Cooking with verjuice.
    New ed.
    Bibliography.
    Includes index.
    ISBN 0 14 300091 8 (pbk.).
    1. Grape juices. 2. Grape products. 3. Cookery, French. I. Title.
641.648

www.penguin.com.au

CONTENTS

CONTENTS

TO PETER WALL,
FOR HAVING FAITH IN THE IDEA

FOREWORD

From time to time every country turns up a leader in its respective arts. In the art of food and the kitchen, Maggie Beer is undoubtedly one of Australia's leading lights. She is a shining example of what can be achieved by vision and doggedness. Her early forays into the subject of verjuice (verjus), until recently little understood in Australia as a cooking condiment, inspired me to imitate her example. I now know of at least eight other wineries producing small amounts of verjuice, and this can only be a good thing for the chefs and cooks of Australia.

In March 1999 Maggie was gracious enough to come to Dromana Estate winery to conduct a highly successful verjuice seminar, held as part of the Melbourne Food and Wine Festival. The seminar and now the publication of this book are part of the ongoing campaign to popularise a very worthwhile addition to the kitchen cupboards of Australia.

For my part, I am pleased to be able to make a small contribution to Maggie's continuing quest, and commend everyone to take up their pans and make verjuice a part of their culinary lives.

GARRY CRITTENDEN
DROMANA ESTATE

ACKNOWLEDGEMENTS

I've long wanted to put down on paper all that I know about verjuice to answer the many questions posed when selling the product in the marketplace. I had envisaged producing pamphlets ourselves, but it was my long-time friend and publisher, Julie Gibbs, who suggested I expand the concept. Julie's gentle nudging has been part of my life for many years and I would have achieved a lot less without her presence, let alone her friendship.

Caroline Pizzey is not only my editor and friend, but she is also my second skin when writing. She questions me when needed and responds to my work to lift me just when it all seems too much. I couldn't imagine writing a book without her.

Thanks go to Garry Crittenden, who joined in my excitement to make verjuice himself and help spread the word. Barbara Santich provided the original benchmark for our verjuice via her 1984 *Winestate* article. I thank her for this and for her research into the use of verjuice in Dijon mustards as well as her continuing scholarship. Special thanks go to Megan Long, who, with the help of Valmai Hankel of the Rare Books section of the State Library of South Australia, uncovered gems of references. ABC Books and Allen & Unwin kindly gave permission to reprint recipes from *A Gondola on the Murray* and *Maggie's Farm* respectively.

Finally, I wish to thank all the chefs, cooks, former staff members, friends and customers who contributed their ideas and recipes to this book. Recording their recipes as well as mine, pulling on the past and thinking of new ideas every day, made writing this book like one huge, very enjoyable brainstorming session.

A HISTORY OF VERJUICE

VERJUICE VERJUS *The acid juice extracted from large unripened grapes, which was formerly widely used as a sauce ingredient, a condiment, and in deglazing. In the Middle Ages, vertjus (literally 'green juice') was an acid-tasting stock prepared with the juice of unripe grapes, sometimes mixed with lemon or sorrel juice, herbs, and spices. It was used in most sauces and liaisons.*

LAROUSSE GASTRONOMIQUE

Although I had always believed verjuice to stem from Roman times, my search for mentions of it as an ingredient has taken me no earlier than the recipes of Taillevent, Frenchman, master cook to King Charles V and the author of *Le Viandier*, published in about 1375.

In *Cod: Biography of a Fish that Changed the World*, Mark Kurlansky gives some of Taillevent's recipes, several of which are for 'Jance', a sauce that reflects the spices of the day. Of the three variations, two have verjuice as the base ingredient. In *Great Cooks and Their Recipes: From Taillevent to Escoffier*, author Anne Willan gives a number of Taillevent's recipes that use verjuice, including barbecued mullet (where verjuice and spices are mixed into a paste that is brushed over the fish), *Civé de veel* (where verjuice is added with vinegar to sharpen a veal stew) and *Hochepot de poullaille* (where verjuice is mixed with cinnamon, cardamom and ginger to flavour a chicken casserole). Willan suggests that 'most writers link medieval cooking with the traditions of ancient Rome, and certainly there are

1

parallels between the recipes of *Le Viandier* and those of the only surviving Roman cookbook, attributed to the epicure Apicius'.

Verjuice was originally thought to be made from the juice of sorrel or sour plums or other unripe fruit and in England from gooseberries, cress and sour crabapples (even today there is a small producer of crabapple verjuice in that country). Maguelonne Toussaint-Samat claims in her *History of Food* that it 'was not until the sixteenth century that anyone thought of using the juice of unripe grapes, crushed and strained, for condimentary purposes . . . outside vine-growing areas the juice of unripe apples or crab apples served the same purpose'. It seems, however, that verjuice made from grapes is the version that has stood the passage of time.

In parts of France, vignerons have long been limited by law to how many tonnes of grapes they can grow per hectare. In order to yield as much fruit as possible, the leaf area to fruit-weight ratio is determined, the idea being to keep the former high so that there are a lot of working leaves for a responsible amount of fruit. If there is too much fruit, the crop is thinned as a vine can only put a certain amount of energy into ripening the fruit. It's easy to see, then, that verjuice could have come about originally as a result of this thinning process, especially considering the 'waste-not-want-not' principle to which early farmers adhered.

It is also possible that verjuice was made when the secondary bunches were handpicked. These small, roundish clusters grow high on the canes and are high in acid but low in sugar and don't ripen properly; if harvested with the rest of the fruit they could potentially lower the overall baumé. (Treating verjuice as a by-product of a secondary crop is perhaps one of the reasons, along with the problem of volatility, that commercial production hasn't occurred in France until very recently – it simply wasn't an economic proposition. As grape-growers, we pick all the grapes for our verjuice early in the season before they are fully ripe, rather than relying on thinnings.)

Ménagier de Paris, a treatise on household management written in

1392, describes verjuice as being traditional to many grape-producing countries, not only France. I have found many references in Italian books to agresto, a sauce made from the juice of unripe grapes. Giacomo Castelvetro suggests in *The Fruit, Herbs and Vegetables of Italy* that every family with an acre of land made at least a barrel of agresto, and goes on to say that the juice may have even been slightly fermented.

Martino of Como, whose recipes appear in the mid-fifteenth-century work *De honesta voluptate* by Platina, 'rarely calls specifically for salt; often lemon juice, verjuice . . . or cheese take its place', writes Anne Willan. A century later, chef Bartolomeo Scappi served his employer Pope Pius IV fried frogs' legs that were accompanied by a sauce made from agresto and egg yolks. (Thickening verjuice with egg yolks seems to have been commonplace: across the seas in early seventeenth-century Britain, Elinor Fettiplace wrote in her 'book of receipts' of beating 'the yelkes of 3 eggs and a little vergis wth some sugger' before adding it to the broth of a boiled chicken.)

As an aside, Paolo Petroni writes in *The Complete Book of Florentine Cooking* 'that tradition endowed this sauce "agresto" with great powers; it was an aphrodisiac, a pain killer, a disinfectant and helped mothers-to-be in giving birth'. What this suggests is that agresto – verjuice – was at one time an entrenched part of Italian life.

Alan Davidson's *Oxford Companion to Food* confirms that verjuice, albeit known by other names, is common to other grape-growing cultures. He writes that abghooreh is a common ingredient in the cuisine of Iran. Here the grapes used, as in France and probably Italy, are the secondary, tiny unripe bunches that grow high on the stalk and are left on the vine after the crop has been picked or the unripe grapes picked to thin out the crop at the beginning of the season. Davidson also mentions that in Lebanon verjuice is known as 'hosrum' and is used in cooking as an alternative to lemon juice.

In medieval Spain, agraz was used in palaces in the preparation of soups, fish and meat. The grapes, grown in the palace gardens and picked the size of chick peas, produced a verjuice much more sour than vinegar, in contrast to the more subtle French version.

However, it was France that held on to verjuice most firmly of all as a way of lending a gentle acidity to food. In the eighteenth century the son of a master vinegar maker became a major force in the mustard industry in Dijon when he instituted a small but revolutionary change by substituting verjuice for vinegar, which made the mustard particularly fine and less acidic and pungent. (The supremacy of Dijon mustard continues today, but despite all efforts it has been impossible to confirm the ingredients used.)

It must be assumed that verjuice has continued to be made by some for domestic use, particularly in wine regions where the tradition of using every part of every food source is strong, as it is in most peasant cultures. Indeed, on a trip to the Dordogne in 1999 I heard about vignerons delivering verjuice to restaurants in barrels, although no one could tell me how it was stabilised. Interestingly, just before publication of the previous edition in 2001 I learned that Javier Ochoa of Bodegas Ochoa, following long academic research and the publication of *Agraz-Verjus: Un Condimento Regio*, had revived production of the sour Spanish agraz in 1998.

However, Paula Wolfert writes in *The Cooking of South-West France* that while verjuice was prominent in old regional cookbooks until the end of the nineteenth century, past that time it has rarely been mentioned. Verjuice, once essential to domestic and professional cooks across Europe, began to fade from sight.

Thank goodness the tide has turned.

MAKING VERJUICE

In my reading of the regional food of France, I found three detailed descriptions of how verjuice is made.

The first is in Elizabeth David's *French Provincial Cooking*: in her meticulous way she has solved the issue of how each household may have been able to make and keep verjuice for later use. She suggests it was a system of pressing the grapes, settling the juice in shallow bowls to allow a scum to form on top (a partial fermentation) and then adding salt to preserve the juice.

The second description comes from *In Madeleine's Kitchen* by Madeleine Kamman. In tackling the problem of volatility, she suggests adding sugar, alcohol and vinegar. As interesting as this would be, I think it would complicate the fresh flavour of the sour-grape juice.

Paula Wolfert provides the third and perhaps most useful description for the home cook in *The Cooking of South-West France*. She suggests that bunches of sour green grapes be dipped into boiling water for 3 seconds to kill the yeasts. The bunches are drained and dried before the grapes are removed from the stem and blended in a food processor. The juice is then strained, and the solids in the sieve are pressed to obtain as much juice as possible.

Wolfert suggests allowing the juice to stand for 10 minutes before straining it again through a muslin cloth and then using it immediately or freezing it.

My method is even simpler. If you have your own grapes, pick them while green, whizz them in a food processor and strain the pulp to collect the juice. Freeze the juice immediately in ice-cube trays and defrost as required.

VERJUICE, THE BAROSSA AND ME

The story of how I came to make verjuice starts well before I'd even heard about this ancient ingredient.

When Colin and I moved to South Australia's Barossa Valley in 1973, we bought an established vineyard and started farming pheasants the same year. In 1977, Colin was awarded a Churchill Fellowship to study game-bird breeding in Europe and the United States. On our return from that trip we decided to open our pheasant farm to the public and built a farm shop alongside the huge dam we had established in those first years in the Valley. I began cooking our produce to sell as a way of teaching customers how to handle game – I had no formal training but I had a lifelong interest in food behind me and was lucky enough to have a natural ability to cook. After a year of doing this, we had the audacity to decide to go one step further and become a restaurant. And so the Pheasant Farm Restaurant was born.

The great strength about living in the country, particularly nearly thirty years ago before refrigerated transport became the norm, was that I had to rely on both my own produce and that of my neighbours. But not having a network of other passionate commercial cooks to turn to created problems in the early days (although there were plenty of keen domestic cooks in the Barossa). The advantage was that I had no option but to develop my own style. I read voraciously and chose books about food that were much more than just a collection of recipes – they tended to be French and, more often than not, were by women.

Women cooks in France at this time were regional cooks – the three-star restaurant was (and still is) a male domain. From these books I learned how to use every conceivable part of every ingredient, from game bird to wild mushroom. I could have had no better education. Foraging for food, whether collecting mushrooms, shooting hares or rabbits, or picking wild plums and olives from roadside trees, is at the heart of country cooking and has long been a Barossa sport. I entered the game with gusto. I also learned from these French women that no part of the vine need be wasted – the leaves, the tendrils, the winter prunings (put aside for year-round grilling) and, of course, the grapes, both ripe and, importantly, unripe.

I can't honestly tell you how many times I came across the magic word 'verjuice' before I looked it up. And then the penny dropped. This was the obvious product for us to make as vignerons and for me to use in the restaurant. As a cook I have that facility of being able to 'taste' what I read about and I knew this was an ingredient I could really embrace. Our break came in 1984: a crisis in the Barossa saw us unable to sell our grapes – making verjuice seemed the next obvious move.

I was very fortunate to have as my ally an equally food-interested friend, Peter Wall, who was then winemaker at Yalumba, an important and historic family winery near Angaston. With his help, and a tonne of unripe Rhine Riesling grapes handpicked during a heatwave, we set about making our first verjuice. The main drawback was that we knew nothing about the production of verjuice other than that the finished product was meant to be tart and acidic – we certainly didn't have examples against which to measure our attempts. None of our reading had turned up anything more – verjuice seemed only to be made by peasant farmers and committed cooks for their own consumption, all using different methods to stabilise the brew. No one seemed to have ever made it commercially.

We certainly didn't get it right first time around: the verjuice wasn't sharp enough and it was volatile, as several exploding bottles taught us.

When historian Barbara Santich reviewed this first batch in *Winestate* she wrote that in fourteenth- and fifteenth-century France 'the flask of verjuice was probably always within the cook's easy reach and as frequently used as soy sauce in a Chinese kitchen today'. Barbara's article became the lynchpin in our production: having used verjuice in France, she was able to provide us with a benchmark and not only headed us in the right direction but encouraged us to continue.

It was at least two years, if not three, before we crushed our next vintage. A tonne of unripe grapes makes a fair bit of verjuice when there are only a handful of cooks using it. By this stage I was not only using verjuice as much as I could in the restaurant but also sending bottles around the countryside for others to trial, among them Stephanie Alexander, Cheong Liew, Janni Kyritsis and Lew Kathreptis.

One year, when verjuice sales had just begun to move, the grapes from our Barossa vineyard were of such a quality and commanding such high prices that we decided instead to use fruit from our warmer Riverland vineyard. It made good economic sense but the result just wasn't the same: the verjuice was thin and tasteless compared to previous years. The worst of it was that we had to wait a whole year before our next Barossa crop was available.

We closed the doors of the Pheasant Farm Restaurant in 1993, burnt out from my inability to delegate at the stoves. Those fourteen glorious years saw us move from a simple 'meal of the day' to a limited à la carte menu. In 1991 we won the *Australian Gourmet Traveller* Remy Martin Restaurant of the Year, judged by the internationally respected food writer Patricia Wells – an extraordinary honour.

When I turned my back on the stoves, Colin and I decided to concentrate on our farm produce, wanting to take it to a different level. By this stage we had our core Pheasant Farm pâté, quince paste and, of course, verjuice. (At the time of writing more than twenty lines are being produced in our state-of-the-art export kitchen, recently extended by the addition of a fully-fledged quince kitchen that has allowed us to enter the global market seriously with all our fruit pastes.)

It was only in 1996, when Adelaide design guru Ian Kidd convinced me to run a back label on our bottles of verjuice, that things really began to take off. This label, he said, should sell our story, just as a wine label does, and should include tips and recipes for people to follow. It was such a simple thing to do, but in all honesty I hadn't thought of it – we were selling to the converted, I thought. All of a sudden I was sharing my knowledge and experience with others, which is very seductive for a cook! Soon afterwards we sent our first consignment to the United Kingdom and Japan. All our patience and hard work was beginning to pay off. (In fact, our verjuice had been used for some time in Tokyo, where chefs teased their apprentices by telling them it was 'pheasant piss' – after all, here was a bottle of sour-grape juice with a flying pheasant on the label. Our new-look labels sorted out any confusion!)

Now our verjuice is being sold worldwide to the discerning cook, and I'm finding more and more ways to use this amazing product (I particularly enjoy hearing from readers via my web site – www.maggiebeer.com.au). The versatility of verjuice seems to know no bounds. Some years we also make a Sangiovese verjuice, which has the same acid balance as our standard verjuice but a touch more fruit, and its attractive pink colour makes it fabulous for desserts. And we have a verjuice mustard in commercial production as well as a ready-made Sangiovese and vanilla bean syrup and, wait for it, an ice-cream (perhaps more of a sorbet) of verjuice and extra-virgin olive oil – we are continually working to value-add our value-adding.

I have been delighted to see more recently other Australians making verjuice, too, in particular Garry Crittenden of Dromana Estate winery on Victoria's Mornington Peninsula, who makes limited quantities each year from Pinot Noir grapes. In 1999 Garry and I shared the platform at a verjuice seminar at his winery, which included crushing the unripe grapes and drinking the beautifully sour juice straight from the basket press. I have since heard of other producers in New South Wales and Victoria's north-east – I am thrilled by this validation of verjuice as a product, and am proud to have started the ball rolling.

But the verjuice revival doesn't stop there. Visiting American winemakers who have stayed with us have gone home to make small quantities, too. And now we are exporting to the United States and Canada. The most wonderful experience of all, however, occurred in France in 1999 when I read of historians, restaurateurs and chefs in Périgord joining forces to reinstate the tradition of making verjuice – they are even doing so in small commercial quantities. The delicious irony for me was that I went on to read that interest had been sparked by verjuice available in Tokyo and the United States. I like to presume, perhaps immodestly, that our role in commercialising verjuice and then exporting it has triggered this revival!

What I do know for certain is that verjuice, indispensable to my cooking for years, is now becoming a necessity for many others. As both vignerons and food producers, our annual production of this product is something of which we are very proud.

Sauces and Condiments

SALSA AGRESTO

VERJUICE VINAIGRETTE FOR OYSTERS

YABBY SAUCE

WARM SEAFOOD DRESSING

CHEAT'S VERJUICE HOLLANDAISE

WALNUT SAUCE FOR PASTA

PICKLED CUMQUATS

PICKLED CUMQUAT AND GREEN PEPPERCORN BUTTER

SALSA AGRESTO

To get into the mood before planning our cooking schools in Tuscany in 1997, Stephanie Alexander and I began by reading Italian cookbooks. I came across a recipe for agresto sauce – a salsa verde finished with sour grape juice (verjuice to me). As it was time for lunch, I looked at what ingredients I had to hand and found lots of walnuts and almonds, loads of parsley and just a little basil – and verjuice, of course. We ate the sauce with toasted bruschetta and Woodside Cheese Wrights' goat's cheese. The result was so fabulous salsa agresto has become a staple in my kitchen – it's great with poached salmon or chicken, too.

The real trick is to add the verjuice just before using the sauce: the sauce turns a brilliant, almost Granny Smith apple green but it oxidises within half an hour.

1 cup almonds
1 cup walnuts
2 cloves garlic
2¾ cups flat-leaf parsley
½ cup basil
1½ teaspoons sea salt
6 grinds black pepper
180 ml extra-virgin olive oil
180 ml verjuice

Preheat the oven to 220°C. Roast the almonds and walnuts separately on baking trays for about 5 minutes, shaking the trays to prevent the nuts from burning. If the walnuts are not fresh season's, rub them in a clean tea towel to remove the bitter skins. Allow to cool.

In a food processor, blend the nuts, garlic, herbs and seasonings to a

14

fine paste with a little of the olive oil. Blend in the balance of the olive oil, then add the verjuice just before serving. The consistency should be perfect for spreading. If required, thin with more verjuice.

MAKES 500 ML

DEMI-GLACE

A sauce Barbara Santich found in her research from the sixteenth and seventeenth centuries could still stand today: reduce equal quantities of verjuice and good, strong stock with finely chopped shallots. Season with salt and pepper and serve with grilled meats.

VERJUICE VINAIGRETTE
FOR OYSTERS

This dressing is amazingly fresh on the palate – try it with oysters, preferably South Australian oysters.

3 tablespoons verjuice
4 tablespoons extra-virgin olive oil
4 shallots, grated
sea salt
freshly ground black pepper
2 dozen freshly shucked oysters

Combine the verjuice, olive oil and shallots in a jar and shake well. Add salt and pepper to taste and spoon over oysters (allow about 1 teaspoon dressing per oyster). Serve immediately.

SERVES 2–4

SIMPLE VINAIGRETTE
Make a simple vinaigrette of 3 parts walnut oil to 1 part verjuice, then add 1 teaspoon Dijon mustard and season with salt and pepper.

The very talented Steve Flamsteed worked part-time for me at the Pheasant Farm for several years while studying oenology at Roseworthy Agricultural College. He went on to win a Queen's Trust Fellowship to study cheesemaking in France, after which he and his brother, Will, opened the King River Café in Victoria's north-east, which became an instant hit. He has left the stoves again to make wine and is now winemaker for YarraBurn in the Yarra Valley.

Steve was one of a small group of extraordinary young people to come through my kitchen at the Pheasant Farm and is a much-loved member of our extended family.

I deglaze the pan with verjuice when cooking almost any sort of poultry, but the most perfect way to use verjuice for me is in a beurre blanc.

When making a beurre blanc, verjuice is way out ahead of any alternative. I think it's because you can reduce it down almost to a syrup that is the right texture to accept the butter. If you do this with wine or vinegar, the result is far too sharp. Beurre blanc made with verjuice is perfectly balanced – a little sweetness, good sharpness and a wonderfully homogenous texture.

Beurre blanc with pan-fried scallops or salmon steaks – sensational!

STEVE FLAMSTEED

YABBY SAUCE

If your guests are too polite to suck the heads when eating freshly boiled yabbies, put the discarded shells aside to make this sauce. Great with freshly boiled yabbies, it also makes a wonderful soup base and when reduced can be tossed through pasta with boiled and peeled yabbies and fresh basil.

40 yabby heads

6 cloves garlic

2 carrots

2 leeks

1 large onion

½ fennel bulb

100 ml extra-virgin olive oil

4 tablespoons Cognac

150 ml tomato paste

500 ml verjuice

sea salt

freshly ground black pepper

60 g unsalted butter (optional)

Crush the yabby heads really well. Dice the garlic and all the vegetables and put them into a saucepan with the yabby heads and olive oil. Sweat until soft, about 15 minutes.

Pour the Cognac into the pan and allow it to evaporate, then mix in the tomato paste. Add the verjuice and simmer gently for 1 hour.

Strain the sauce into a clean saucepan through a conical sieve or similar, pushing on the contents as you do so to extract as much flavour as possible. Reduce the sauce to the desired consistency, then season and add the butter to make it more velvety, if desired.

This sauce should be used as soon as possible but can be stored for a couple of days in a very cold refrigerator.

MAKES 500 ML

WARM SEAFOOD DRESSING

We make this dressing to partner my salmon custards or even the mushroom and capsicum pâté, but it is especially good with poached fish or grilled shellfish.

125 ml verjuice
juice of 1 lemon
1 shallot, finely sliced
sea salt
freshly ground black pepper
120 ml extra-virgin olive oil
1 tablespoon freshly plucked chervil

Reduce the verjuice, lemon juice and shallot over heat until 4 tablespoons liquid remain. Remove the pan from the heat, then season with salt and pepper and add the olive oil. Swirl in the chervil and use immediately.

MAKES 200 ML

WALNUT OIL VINAIGRETTE
Make a vinaigrette of 2 tablespoons verjuice, 2 teaspoons lemon juice, 125 ml walnut oil, salt and pepper. Toss this through a salad of bitter greens, freshly shelled walnuts, roasted garlic and grapes, if they are in season.

CHEAT'S VERJUICE

HOLLANDAISE

I prefer using verjuice in hollandaise than the more usual vinegar as I think it gives the sauce a rounder finish. And I love using my food processor to make hollandaise!

150 g unsalted butter
4 egg yolks
2 tablespoons verjuice
lemon juice (optional)
freshly ground white *or* black pepper

Melt the butter in a heavy-based saucepan (preferably one without a black base – one lined with white enamel is best of all) and cook it until nut-brown, making sure you don't burn it.

Whizz the egg yolks and verjuice in a food processor, then using a funnel, pour in the hot butter while the motor is running. Leave the residue in the pan (I've allowed for the wastage). Taste the sauce and adjust with a squeeze of lemon juice, if needed, then add some pepper (white if you're a purist; black if you're like me and that's all there is in the house).

Pour the hollandaise into a jug or bowl ready to serve. If you're not using the sauce immediately, press a piece of plastic film down onto the surface to prevent a skin from forming. Serve with fresh asparagus.

MAKES ABOUT 250 ML

WALNUT SAUCE FOR PASTA

Toss this versatile sauce through pasta with olive oil, parsley and parmesan, or serve it alongside grilled or poached chicken or rabbit, or scoop it onto bruschetta. Walnuts are more prone to rancidity than almost any other food I know – roasting them first will help avoid disappointment.

150 g freshly shelled walnuts
2 cloves garlic
sea salt
1 slice good-quality white bread
(wood-fired, if available)
100 ml verjuice
walnut oil
freshly ground black pepper
flat-leaf parsley

Preheat the oven to 220°C. Dry-roast the walnuts on a baking tray in the oven for about 10 minutes, shaking the tray occasionally to prevent the nuts from burning. If the walnuts are not fresh season's, rub them in a clean tea towel while still hot to remove the bitter skins. Allow to cool.

Crush the garlic cloves and a little salt with the blade of a large knife. Remove the crusts from the bread and discard. Break the bread into pieces and spread with the crushed garlic, then soak it for a few minutes in half the verjuice.

Carefully grind the walnuts in a food processor, pulsing only. Add the soaked bread and garlic and process to a paste. With the motor running, slowly add 70 ml walnut oil, as if making mayonnaise, then add the remaining verjuice and adjust the seasoning. Serve tossed through pasta with flat-leaf parsley and a drizzle of walnut oil.

SERVES 2–4

21

PICKLED CUMQUATS

When we were offered a large quantity of cumquats to pickle, the staff at Charlick's collaborated on the recipe. It was their idea, in fact, to use verjuice to mellow the effect of the vinegar. I give the original quantities here, as pickled cumquats are hard to find and many restaurant cooks have use for them.

As they are not cooked, the pickled cumquats retain a wonderful crispness and, given time, the flavour of the syrup permeates the flesh.

10 kg cumquats with tiny stems
    attached
5 kg castor sugar
1 litre verjuice
2 litres white wine
7 litres white vinegar
30 cloves
10 cinnamon sticks
20 cardamom pods

Wash and drain the cumquats. Put the castor sugar and all the liquids into a large stainless steel pot and bring to a simmer, stirring to dissolve the sugar. Add the spices and simmer for 5 minutes. Pack the cumquats into sterilised jars and pour in the hot syrup. Seal when cool and leave to mature for a few months.

PORCINI AND VERJUICE
Reconstitute dried porcini in verjuice for 24 hours. Use the strained liquid in sauces.

PICKLED CUMQUAT AND GREEN
PEPPERCORN BUTTER

Melt a slice of this delicious butter on fish as it grills, or add it to the parcel before wrapping and baking fish. For the best flavour, look for a good-quality, unsalted cultured butter.

60 g green peppercorns
verjuice
750 ml duck *or* chicken stock
600 g Pickled Cumquats
    (see page 22)
1 head of garlic
1 kg softened unsalted cultured
    butter
1 cup finely chopped flat-leaf parsley
½ teaspoon finely ground black
    pepper

Soak the peppercorns in a little verjuice at least overnight to rid them of any briny flavour (the peppercorns can, in fact, be stored indefinitely like this). Meanwhile, reduce the stock over high heat until 200 ml remains. Allow to cool. Next day, seed and chop the pickled cumquats. Finely chop the garlic. Whiz the butter in a food processor until pale and soft. Add the remaining ingredients, except the stock, pulsing as you go, then add the stock.

Divide the mixture into manageable amounts, then roll into logs and wrap in foil. The butter will keep for up to 2 weeks in the refrigerator if wrapped well.

Vegetables

ALMOND AND GARLIC SOUP WITH GRAPES

GREEN SALAD WITH WALNUTS AND VERJUICE

BRAISED GREEN OLIVES WITH ROASTED ALMONDS

GRILLED VEGETABLES IN A VERJUICE AND OLIVE OIL BATH

ROASTED MUSHROOMS

CULTIVATED MUSHROOMS IN VINE LEAVES WITH VERJUICE

VINE LEAVES FILLED WITH GOAT'S CHEESE AND WALNUTS

ZUCCHINI IN AGRODOLCE

WARM SALAD OF WAXY POTATOES AND BEANS

GNOCCHI WITH BURNT BUTTER, VERJUICE AND PARSLEY

OMELETTE WITH SORREL AND ANCHOVY

SALAD OF TRUFFLED EGGS WITH VERJUICE

POTATOES WITH CAPERS

POT-ROASTED ARTICHOKES

ALMOND AND GARLIC SOUP
WITH GRAPES

The combination of almonds, garlic and grapes makes this a brilliantly refreshing yet rich cold soup for a summer's luncheon. The soup is made a little like a mayonnaise, and ice cubes of verjuice are stirred in just before serving. The grapes are best added at the table as they sink to the bottom very quickly. The sight of the bobbing grapes is worth it!

Choose green sultana grapes rather than yellow ones, which will be overripe for this dish. And look for a mellow olive oil rather than an aggressive green one.

250 g stale French stick
cold milk
750 ml verjuice
150 g almonds
2 large cloves garlic
2 tablespoons white-wine vinegar
125 ml mellow extra-virgin olive oil
sea salt
200 g sultana grapes

Pour the verjuice into ice-cube trays and put into the freezer.

Preheat the oven to 220°C. Soak the bread in the milk for 20 minutes, then squeeze it lightly to remove the milk.

Roast the almonds on a baking tray for about 5 minutes, shaking the tray to prevent the nuts from burning. Allow to cool.

Put the bread, almonds, garlic and vinegar into a food processor and blend, adding the oil slowly until the mixture has amalgamated. Add salt if necessary. Refrigerate until well chilled.

To serve, pour the soup into shallow bowls, then add the verjuice ice cubes and grapes and serve immediately.

SERVES 4

BRAISED FENNEL

Slowly braise fennel in verjuice, turning it frequently, then reduce the cooking liquid to a syrupy glaze. Remove from the heat and swirl in extra-virgin olive oil and freshly chopped flat-leaf parsley.

GREEN SALAD WITH WALNUTS
AND VERJUICE

Walnuts, grapes and verjuice are a natural combination, so using walnut oil and verjuice in a vinaigrette makes sense. But taste the oil first to check how bold the flavour is. If the salad leaves are very young and delicate, temper the walnut oil by combining it with a little light olive oil.

6 handfuls salad greens
freshly shelled walnuts
1 clove garlic

VINAIGRETTE
2 tablespoons verjuice
2 teaspoons lemon juice
sea salt
125 ml walnut oil
freshly ground black pepper

Preheat the oven to 220°C. Wash and dry the salad greens and set them aside. Roast the walnuts on a baking tray for about 5 minutes, shaking the tray to prevent the nuts from burning. If the walnuts are not fresh season's, rub them in a clean tea towel to remove the bitter skins. Allow to cool.

Rub the cut clove of garlic over the inside of a salad bowl and discard.

To make the vinaigrette, whisk the verjuice and lemon juice with a little sea salt. Slowly whisk in the oil until blended, then season with pepper. Toss the salad greens and walnuts with the vinaigrette until lightly but evenly coated. A handful of fresh green grapes would be an appropriate addition, too.

SERVES 6

BRAISED GREEN OLIVES WITH
ROASTED ALMONDS

This recipe came about after friend and colleague Sophie Zalokar, who helped me so much with the food for Maggie's Table, *asked me to put together some food to feature in her first book,* PicNic. *The following is a happy marriage of great ingredients, inspired by the fact that Sophie and I love to cook things alike.*

120 g almonds (skins on)
450 g green olives
100 ml verjuice
100 ml water
2 strips lemon zest
2 sprigs thyme
1 bay leaf
125 ml extra-virgin olive oil

Preheat the oven to 220°C. Dry-roast the almonds on a baking tray in the oven for about 5 minutes, shaking the tray occasionally to prevent the nuts from burning. Set aside to cool.

Put all the ingredients except for the almonds and olive oil into a small baking dish. Press a sheet of baking paper down onto the olive mixture and cover the dish tightly with foil. Braise in the oven for 1 hour, then remove and allow the olives to cool a little in the juices.

Strain off the liquid, then toss the olives with the almonds and olive oil and serve warm.

SERVES 6

GRILLED VEGETABLES IN A
VERJUICE AND OLIVE OIL BATH

Brushing a mixture of verjuice and olive oil onto mushrooms before grilling them has long been a favourite technique of mine, so it seemed natural to extend this process to making a 'bath' for the hot, grilled vegetables to rest in. The vegetables take up the flavour of the vinaigrette and release their own juices – particularly the red capsicum and onion – just as resting meat does.

Try adding fried haloumi cheese, finely sliced baby bocconcini, fresh ricotta or goat's curd to the resting vegetables and then toss with rocket as a salad or through pasta as a substantial meal.

3 red onions

2 baby fennel bulbs

150 ml extra-virgin olive oil

leaves from 2 sprigs thyme

1 meyer lemon, thinly sliced

2 red capsicums

1 eggplant

2 zucchini

75 ml verjuice

sea salt

freshly ground black pepper

Preheat the barbecue grill to hot. Remove the outer skins from the onions and fennel, then cut the onions into quarters and the fennel in half lengthwise. Mix the olive oil with the thyme and lemon, then toss all the vegetables in this mixture until just coated. Reserve any leftover olive oil mixture.

Transfer the oiled vegetables to the hot grill. While they are cooking, combine the verjuice and the reserved olive oil mixture in a large baking dish and season to taste. Remove the vegetables from the grill as they are ready: cooking times will vary depending on the kind of vegetable and the size of each piece. Put the grilled vegetables into the verjuice 'bath' to rest while the remaining vegetables cook (peel away the blackened skin on the capsicum pieces before adding it to the bath).

Serve warm as a side dish or on a bed of soft polenta as a main meal. Be sure to drizzle each serving with plenty of the delicious juices!

SERVES 4

ZUCCHINI WITH VERJUICE AND CHIVES
Trim the ends from tiny young zucchini and boil them whole for 3–4 minutes, then drain and allow to cool enough to be able to handle them. Cut into long strips and toss with freshly chopped chives and 4 parts extra-virgin olive oil to 1 part verjuice. Season.

ROASTED MUSHROOMS

These mushrooms are great with beef; on good, grilled bread alongside eggs; or tossed through pasta.

400 g field mushrooms
400 g Swiss brown mushrooms
175 ml verjuice
1 tablespoon finely chopped
   parsley stalks
1 tablespoon freshly chopped
   oregano
sea salt
freshly ground black pepper
extra parsley
extra-virgin olive oil (optional)

Preheat the oven to 180°C. Cut all the mushrooms into quarters and transfer to a large, shallow baking dish. Combine the remaining ingredients except the extra parsley and the olive oil and pour over the mushrooms. Roast the mushrooms until cooked through – this may take up to an hour. Transfer the dish to the stove and reduce the cooking liquid by three-quarters. Finish with a sprinkling of chopped parsley and a little olive oil to moisten the dish, if required.

SERVES 6

GRILLED WILD MUSHROOMS
Grill wild mushrooms brushed with verjuice and walnut oil on the barbecue, then drizzle with more verjuice and season. Even more delicious if grilled over vine cuttings!

Italian-born Stefano de Pieri, now known across Australia for his tel-
evision series and books A Gondola on the Murray, *volumes 1 and 2,*
is an inspiration, and not only in his kitchens at the Grand Hotel in
Mildura, Victoria. He is also responsible for initiating the wonderful
Mildura Writers' Festival: I make sure I go every year – it is a fantas-
tic mix of good writing (especially poetry), good food and good fun.

We have been friends from the day we met quite some years ago
now, which is how I found myself in his kitchen at the Grand cook-
ing a supper for 200 people during the festival. I'll never forget
making polenta for that crowd in one large pot! What fun it is work-
ing for a commonly held cause, such as supporting a regional
community, with like-minded people. Stefano has certainly returned
the favour for me in many ways, perhaps most of all by using verjuice
so enthusiastically in his famous risottos in his Cantinetta.

I use verjuice instead of white wine, which I find too acerbic.
I love it because it has the fragrance of kaffir lime leaves –
lemony but not acidic. This makes verjuice great with fish of
all kinds, and poultry, too, but I find it best of all in risotto
bases instead of wine, a signature of mine. I also drink Maggie's verjuice with chilled water!

STEFANO DE PIERI

CULTIVATED MUSHROOMS IN VINE LEAVES WITH VERJUICE

The inspiration for this dish was a recipe in Elizabeth David's An Omelette and a Glass of Wine. *My version uses vine leaves blanched in verjuice. I served this dish in the Pheasant Farm Restaurant as an accompaniment to rabbit, in particular, when wild mushrooms were not in season and I wanted to add an earthiness that cultivated mushrooms couldn't provide. The vine leaves and verjuice give a wonderful dimension to these mushrooms – it's as if you have picked your own from the paddock!*

6 cloves garlic

150 ml extra-virgin olive oil

200 ml verjuice

12 fresh young vine leaves

300 g flat cultivated mushrooms
    (about 12)

1 teaspoon sea salt

freshly ground black pepper

Preheat the oven to 220°C. Slowly caramelise the garlic cloves in 1 tablespoon of the olive oil in a saucepan over a gentle heat.

Bring the verjuice to a boil in an enamelled or stainless steel saucepan, then blanch the vine leaves by immersing them one at a time and drain well. Reserve the verjuice.

Line a small ovenproof dish with 6 of the vine leaves. Drizzle a little of the olive oil over, then arrange a layer of mushrooms, followed by some of the garlic, a pinch of the salt and a turn of the pepper grinder and another drizzle of the oil.

Add another layer of mushrooms and repeat the procedure. Top with the remaining vine leaves and drizzle over the last of the olive oil. Bake for 25 minutes. While still hot, drizzle 2 tablespoons of the reserved verjuice over the dish to create a vinaigrette.

Both the leaves and mushrooms are eaten – and leftovers are very good refrigerated for the next day.

SERVES 6

PASTA WITH ZUCCHINI FLOWERS AND CURRANTS
Soak currants in verjuice for 20 minutes, then drain. Cook quartered zucchini flowers in extra-virgin olive oil in a covered pan until softened. Warm the currants in more oil with pine nuts and anchovies and toss through hot pasta with the zucchini flowers, lots of flat-leaf parsley, salt and pepper.

VINE LEAVES FILLED WITH GOAT'S CHEESE AND WALNUTS

Here verjuice is used to blanch vine leaves that are then wrapped around goat's cheese studded with walnuts. These little parcels are then grilled, baked or barbecued – perfect autumn fare.

12 freshly shelled walnuts
200 ml verjuice
12 fresh young vine leaves
2 tablespoons flat-leaf parsley leaves
300 g fresh goat's cheese
good-quality walnut oil
sea salt
freshly ground black pepper

Preheat the oven to 220°C. Dry-roast the walnuts for 6–8 minutes, shaking the tray to prevent the nuts from burning. If the walnuts are not fresh season's, rub them in a clean tea towel to remove the bitter skins. Set aside to cool.

Bring the verjuice to a boil in an enamelled or stainless steel saucepan. Blanch the vine leaves by immersing them one at a time and drain well. Reserve the verjuice.

Roughly chop the walnuts and parsley and mix them into the goat's cheese. Form the cheese into a log (if necessary, refrigerate it to firm it up a bit). Cut the log into 12 even pieces and wrap each in a vine leaf. Brush each parcel with walnut oil, then season with salt and pepper and grill seam-side down on a barbecue or a chargrill pan or bake at 220°C for 4 minutes to warm the cheese.

Make a vinaigrette with walnut oil and some of the reserved verjuice and spoon it over the warmed parcels. Serve with crusty bread.

SERVES 4

VINE LEAF AND CHEESE ROLLS

Blanch young vine leaves in boiling verjuice in a non-reactive pan until they just change colour. Make them into tiny rolls with blue cheese and walnuts or goat's cheese and walnuts or roasted pine nuts. Cook in a hot oven for a few minutes dotted with a little butter and seasoned with salt and pepper.

Janni Kyritsis, until mid-2002 the chef and partner at Sydney's highly successful MG Garage (awarded the Remy Martin Cognac/Australian Gourmet Traveller Restaurant of the Year in 2000), has been associated with Australia's finest restaurants over his long career, including Stephanie's, Berowra Waters and Bennelong. It was Janni who was the catalyst for our verjuice being put into flagons for a few vintages: he was so enthusiastic about verjuice that he suggested the idea to us for restaurant kitchens. We've now discontinued it, and feel that the flagons didn't work because they were heavy and cumbersome – so often verjuice is needed as a quick splash and therefore needs to be easy to get at. Not every idea works, but feedback is important in any product development – and for Janni I'd have a go at almost anything!

I use verjuice in quite a few ways. I use it to poach food as it has a good balance of acidity and sweetness and is a natural ingredient available at my fingertips.

A favourite dish at MG Garage was sautéd blond Barossa Chook livers with boned and crumbed chicken feet. After pan-frying the livers, I deglazed the pan with verjuice – wine would have been too harsh – and added a nut of butter at the end. The creaminess of the livers, the acidity of the verjuice and the crunchiness of the chicken feet – all served with a delicate salad of greens – made for a fabulous dish.

But above all I use verjuice in my salad dressings. Today we have all learned to use tender baby greens with delicate flavours – it is a crime, then, to use a heavy vinegar such as balsamic. Verjuice provides the perfect balance between acidity and sweetness without overpowering the baby leaves. I use it in equal quantities with a non-aggressive olive oil.

JANNI KYRITSIS

ZUCCHINI IN AGRODOLCE

I found this recipe in Elizabeth David's Italian Food, *but prefer to use verjuice rather than white-wine vinegar and sugar. Look for small zucchini for this dish.*

450 g small zucchini

salt

4 tablespoons fruity extra-virgin
   olive oil

freshly ground black pepper

pinch of ground cinnamon

3 tablespoons verjuice

Cut the zucchini into thick rounds, then salt lightly and drain for 1 hour. Rinse the zucchini and dry well with kitchen paper. Heat the olive oil in a large frying pan with a lid and gently cook the zucchini, covered, for about 5 minutes, then remove the lid and season with pepper and cinnamon and check for salt. Turn up the heat and add the verjuice, then cook for a few minutes more until the sauce is syrupy. Serve immediately with grilled fish or pan-fried chicken breasts.

SERVES 4

BUTTERY SPINACH
Cook spinach in butter, then add a grinding of pepper, a grating of nutmeg and a dash of verjuice.

WARM SALAD OF WAXY POTATOES

AND BEANS

Try this in December when the early, sweet small beans arrive at the same time as the first of the pink-eyes from Tasmania (in Hobart they're said to be best of all by Christmas Day). The verjuice dressing is an excellent foil to the richness of really good waxy potatoes.

This salad makes a great entrée or luncheon dish. You can add pancetta if you want to make a more substantial meal.

200 g freshly shelled walnuts

125 ml good-quality walnut oil

2 tablespoons verjuice

generous squeeze of lemon juice

2 tablespoons cream

sea salt

freshly ground black pepper

500 g thin green beans

500 g small waxy potatoes

Preheat the oven to 220°C. Dry-roast the walnuts for 6–8 minutes, shaking the tray to prevent the nuts from burning. If the walnuts are not fresh season's, rub them in a clean tea towel to remove the bitter skins. Set aside to cool.

Make a vinaigrette by mixing the walnut oil, verjuice and lemon juice, then add the cream and season. Set aside.

Trim the beans if necessary. Put 2 saucepans of water on to boil.

Boil the potatoes in salted water in one of the saucepans for about 15–20 minutes until cooked, then drain immediately.

Salt the other saucepan of boiling water, then cook the beans for 5 minutes so they are still a little al dente. Drain the beans and allow them to cool slightly.

Cut the warm potatoes in half and toss with the vinaigrette, walnuts and beans and serve immediately.

SERVES 6–8

BAKED OLIVES

Toss 2 cups oil-cured olives, 2 finely chopped garlic cloves and the zest of an orange cut into strips with extra-virgin olive oil, then sprinkle with verjuice. Bake at 180°C for about 10 minutes and allow to cool just a little before serving. Moisten with a little more of the oil and verjuice, if necessary.

GNOCCHI WITH BURNT BUTTER, VERJUICE, PARMESAN AND PARSLEY

Alex Herbert came to me in the last six months of the Pheasant Farm: without her drive, energy and perfectionist streak we would never have coped with the public onslaught that began once word was out we were closing. I'm indebted to her for her commitment at what was the end of a long road for me. Alex went on to open her own restaurant, Bird Cow Fish, in Sydney, before setting up De'lish, a deli with a real difference. No longer involved there, Alex will without doubt have more exciting projects ahead of her. This is her recipe.

water

sea salt

40 g unsalted butter

1 tablespoon olive oil

verjuice

freshly ground black pepper

1 tablespoon freshly chopped
    flat-leaf parsley

freshly shaved Parmigiano-Reggiano

GNOCCHI

1.5 kg desiree potatoes

1 × 55 g egg

2 teaspoons sea salt

2 tablespoons freshly grated grana
    padano *or* Parmigiano-Reggiano

125 g plain flour

To begin making the gnocchi, put the potatoes, with their skins on, into a saucepan of cold water and bring to a boil. Simmer gently until done, about 20 minutes. The potatoes must not be over- or undercooked. Test with a skewer to be sure – when it is easily inserted, the potato is cooked. Avoid testing the potatoes too frequently or you risk them becoming waterlogged.

Drain the potatoes in a colander, then put the colander over the saucepan the potatoes were cooked in and cover with a clean tea towel. Set aside in a warm place for 10 minutes. This allows the potatoes to dry off.

Peel the potatoes and put them in batches through a food mill or potato ricer – do this back into the dried cooking pot. Gently mix the egg, salt and parmesan into the potato, then sift in the flour and combine the mixture with a few swift folds.

Tip the potato mixture onto a lightly floured bench and gently work it into a smooth, homogenous mound. Scrape down the bench and wash and dry your hands. Lightly flour the bench again. Cut off a quarter of the dough and roll it into a sausage 3 cm thick. Cut the sausage into

2 cm lengths. Repeat with the remaining dough. You should end up with about 60 gnocchi. Put them on a tray lined with greaseproof paper until ready to cook.

Bring a large pot of salted water to a boil. When ready to cook the gnocchi, heat the butter in a wide frying pan, taking it to a nut-brown colour, then add the olive oil to inhibit burning and remove from the heat.

Tip a third of the gnocchi into the boiling water in one movement. Shortly after the gnocchi have risen to the surface, test for doneness and remove with a strainer and drain. Repeat with the remaining gnocchi.

Reheat the butter until sizzling, then add the drained gnocchi and a good splash of verjuice. Season with salt and pepper and add the parsley. Tip the gnocchi onto serving plates and top with Parmigiano-Reggiano.

SERVES 6

OMELETTE WITH SORREL
AND ANCHOVY

Verjuice and sorrel have a natural affinity – both have a lemony tang that combines beautifully with cream. In this recipe, the anchovy rounds out the flavour even further.

30 g unsalted butter
3 eggs
pinch of salt
freshly ground black pepper
1 anchovy fillet
1 good handful young sorrel leaves
2 tablespoons cream
2 tablespoons verjuice
squeeze of lemon juice (optional)

Melt half the butter and allow it to cool a little. Break the eggs into a bowl, then add the melted butter with the salt and a grinding of pepper and beat lightly with a fork. Set aside.

Finely chop the anchovy and trim and chop the sorrel. Reduce the cream and verjuice by half in a small enamelled or stainless steel saucepan, then add the anchovy and sorrel. Check the seasoning, adding a squeeze of lemon juice if required. The sorrel will form its own purée in just a few minutes. Keep warm.

Melt the remaining butter in an omelette pan, coating the base with the butter as it melts. When the butter is nut-brown, pour in the eggs, stirring quickly with a fork to distribute the mixture. Lift the edge gently as it cooks to allow more mixture to run underneath. The omelette must by shiny and very moist in the centre. When the egg is almost cooked, spoon the warm sorrel mixture into the centre, then turn the omelette onto itself as you slide it onto a warmed plate.

Rub an extra bit of butter over the top – it melts in wonderfully! Serve immediately.

SERVES 1

TINY BARBECUED ONIONS
Boil pearl or small pickling onions in their skins for about 2 minutes, then drain and peel. Cook the onions in verjuice with a few whole peppercorns and fresh bay leaves until softened but still holding their shape and set aside for the flavours to mature. Thread the onions onto skewers with fresh bay leaves and barbecue.

SALAD OF TRUFFLED EGGS
WITH VERJUICE

Late December means fresh truffles, imported by Simon Johnson in Sydney. By carefully storing them for a short while in a jar with uncooked whole eggs, you will find that the eggs take on the flavour of the truffles quite wonderfully. One day, out of the blue, my friend Damien Pignolet faxed me this recipe for a salad that he and his wife, Julie, shared for brunch. It came with the note: 'I thought you might like this for the next time you have truffles on hand! I love your verjuice and it brings out a magical quality in this salad.' The recipe could easily feed four if served with croutons. The herb called salad burnet is a welcome addition, if you have it – it adds a wonderful depth and freshness.

1 clove garlic, smashed

2 teaspoons Dijon mustard

3 tablespoons crème fraîche

verjuice

squeeze of lemon juice (optional)

salt

freshly ground black pepper

4 eggs perfumed with fresh truffles

shaved truffle

organic iceberg lettuce, washed

freshly chopped chives

Rub a salad bowl with the smashed garlic and discard the clove. Mix the mustard and crème fraîche in the bowl and add verjuice to taste (add a squeeze of lemon juice, if necessary), then season. Set aside.

Poach the eggs in 9 parts water to 1 part verjuice until still rather soft, then transfer them with a slotted spoon to the dressing. Shake the bowl to coat the eggs.

Shave some truffle over the eggs, then break the lettuce into the bowl and add pepper and a few chopped chives. Toss carefully, although the eggs are meant to break up. Serve immediately.

SERVES 2–4

TRUFFLED RISOTTO

The exotic perfume of truffles can be achieved in a risotto by storing a truffle with arborio rice for a day or two and then making the risotto in the usual way. All you will need is Parmigiano-Reggiano, a good knob of butter and a splash of verjuice to release the truffle flavour. Don't forget freshly ground pepper.

POTATOES WITH CAPERS

*I cooked this dish for a huge group of people at an olive oil conference.
With only a tiny electric stove, we had to cook the food in waves, and
a lot of ingenuity was required. One of the helpers gave me the tip of
bringing the water and potatoes to a boil, then turning off the heat and
allowing the potatoes to sit in the water, covered with a tight lid, off
the stove. The potatoes cooked to perfection and were still hot, yet not
too hot to handle, as I drained and cut them in half.*

*Look for waxy potatoes for this dish – kipfler, patrone, bintje or
Tasmanian pink-eyes would all be good choices.*

1 kg small waxy potatoes, washed
   well
2 tablespoons verjuice
4 tablespoons extra-virgin olive oil
¼ cup roughly chopped flat-leaf
   parsley
2 tablespoons small capers
freshly ground black pepper
sea salt (optional)

Boil the potatoes until they are
tender, then drain. Toss the pan
over heat for a moment to dry the
potatoes thoroughly, then sprinkle
in the verjuice and allow it to
sizzle. Cut the warm potatoes in
half (this ensures they absorb the
dressing) and return them to the
pan. Add the other ingredients
and toss well. Turn into a hot
dish and serve.

SERVES 6

POT-ROASTED ARTICHOKES

This dish is spectacularly simple and requires nothing more as an accompaniment than a loaf of really good bread.

4–6 artichokes
125 ml verjuice
peeled shallots *or* peeled garlic cloves
    (optional)
250 ml extra-virgin olive oil
sea salt
freshly ground black pepper
freshly chopped flat-leaf parsley

Prepare the artichokes by cutting away the top third and then removing the tough outer leaves to reveal the yellowy-green ones below. Cut each artichoke into quarters and extract the hairy choke with a teaspoon. As you finish preparing each artichoke, immediately toss it in the verjuice to avoid discoloration, making sure you coat all surfaces.

Heat the olive oil gently in a heavy-based non-reactive pan 15–18 cm in diameter. Add shallots or garlic, if desired. Lift the artichokes out of the verjuice and seal on both sides in the oil. Strain 3 tablespoons of the verjuice into the pan. Bring the artichokes and their vinaigrette to a simmer and cook for 25 minutes, turning several times. Season and stir through plenty of parsley. Serve warm or at room temperature with crusty bread.

SERVES 2–3

Fish and Shellfish

BLUE SWIMMER CRAB RISOTTO WITH VERJUICE

PASTA WITH CLAM AND VERJUICE SAUCE

COFFIN BAY SCALLOPS WITH VERJUICE BUTTER SAUCE

SCALLOPS WITH SEA-URCHIN BUTTER

SALMON IN VERJUICE FOR A PARTY

MORETON BAY BUGS WOK-SEARED WITH CITRUS

SKATE WITH CAPERS AND OLIVES

TUNA ROLLS WITH CURRANTS, PINE NUTS AND BAY LEAVES

CARPACCIO OF WILD BARRAMUNDI WITH RED GRAPES

OYSTERS WITH LEEKS AND VERJUICE

WARM SALAD OF RED FIN

STUFFED TROUT WITH VERJUICE SAUCE

OCEAN TROUT IN VERJUICE JELLY

BLUE SWIMMER CRAB RISOTTO
WITH VERJUICE

A cook who uses what's to hand leaves herself open to making discoveries – as I did when I opened the fridge looking for wine for a risotto to find an open bottle of verjuice instead. I rarely use wine now!

500 g handpicked fresh blue
    swimmer crabmeat
sea salt
freshly ground black pepper
extra-virgin olive oil (optional)
squeeze of lemon juice (optional)
1.25 litres jellied fish *or* crab stock
2 large brown onions
225 g unsalted butter
500 g arborio rice
175 ml verjuice
2 lemons, quartered
¼ cup coriander leaves

If you have bought vacuum-packed crabmeat, transfer it to a dish and season with salt and pepper and drizzle it with olive oil and lemon juice to allow plastic smell to dissipate. Bring the stock to a simmer in a saucepan.

Finely chop the onions and sweat them in 150 g of the butter in a heavy-based saucepan. Add the rice, stirring well until it is coated with butter. When the rice is glistening, turn up the heat and stir in the verjuice and let it evaporate.

Ladle in some hot stock and stir until it has been absorbed. Continue adding the stock a ladleful at a time, stirring frequently, until the rice is cooked but still firm – this will take about 20 minutes.

A few minutes before the rice is cooked, season the risotto lightly with salt, then add the remaining

butter and gently fold in the crabmeat, taking care not to break it up. Serve this lovely, rich risotto with wedges of lemon alongside and a grinding of black pepper.

SERVES 6

TOMMY RUFF SALAD

Make a hot vinaigrette to use with Tommy ruffs or any other quite fatty fish. Sauté lots of chopped red onion in extra-virgin olive oil, then add lemon juice, fresh bay leaves and currants reconstituted in verjuice and allow to sweat. Add 1 part verjuice to 4 parts extra-virgin olive oil away from the heat and season with salt and pepper. The thickness of the fish will determine whether you use it raw or whether you dust it with seasoned flour and just seal it in nut-brown butter and a little oil. Pour the hot vinaigrette over the fish and allow to cool to room temperature before serving.

PASTA WITH CLAM AND
VERJUICE SAUCE

Once the water for the pasta is boiling, this deliciously simple dish can be pulled together in 10 minutes.

200 g dried spaghettini

sea salt

1 kg clams

250 ml verjuice

wild fennel *or* 1 teaspoon
    fennel seeds

125 ml extra-virgin olive oil

1 clove garlic, minced

1 cup freshly plucked flat-leaf parsley

freshly ground black pepper

Bring a large pot of salted water to a boil and cook the spaghettini for the time advised by the manufacturer. Meanwhile, scrub the clams thoroughly and tip them into a heavy-based, wide pot that has a tight-fitting lid. Pour in the verjuice and snip a few pieces of wild fennel over the clams (or sprinkle in the fennel seeds). Cover with the lid and stand the pot over a high heat, shaking it for a few minutes until the clams open.

Strain the juices from the pot, in case of grit, then return them with the clams to the pot and add the olive oil, garlic and parsley. Season with pepper and toss through the drained pasta. Serve with crusty bread to mop up the juices.

SERVES 2

I first met Philippe Mouchel over the phone when he was at Melbourne's Paul Bocuse Restaurant and buying for the Daimaru food hall – not only was he one of the first chefs to use my verjuice, he was also the first person to order it to be sold at retail. That was all a long time ago, but I'll be forever grateful for his commitment. Perhaps his French background made verjuice a natural ingredient for him to seek out.

A good verjuice, I believe, finds a balance between sweetness and acidity, with the acidity being slightly more prominent. I used Maggie Beer's verjuice when it was first released – I am in fact still using it!

I particularly like serving slow-roasted salmon with a verjuice beurre blanc. But I do not limit the use of verjuice to fish. It works equally well with duck, guinea fowl or even foie gras, where I use verjuice to finish the dish after pan-frying.

I find adding verjuice to a sauce or jus at the last minute maintains its characteristic flavour. Adding a drop of vinegar to the dish also enhances the verjuice flavour. When possible, I like to add a few grapes to the sauce as a garnish.

PHILIPPE MOUCHEL

COFFIN BAY SCALLOPS WITH VERJUICE BUTTER SAUCE

In 1991 Urs Inauen, Cheong Liew, Tom Milligan, Nigel Hopkins and I won the Seppelts Menu of the Year competition, the prize for which took us to New York. It was while we were practising our menu that Tom, then of the Hyatt in Adelaide, discovered that a verjuice reduction not only tastes wonderful but also accepts butter much more readily than the more usual vinegar reduction used when making a beurre blanc. (For the uninitiated, making a traditional beurre blanc can be fraught with difficulties as the sauce has a tendency to split while the butter is being added.)

It takes only a few minutes to pull this dish together as long as everything is ready: the verjuice reduction should be hot and the butter for the sauce cold; the pan for the scallops should be hot and the butter at the nut-brown stage. If you think the timing is going to put too much pressure on you, preheat the oven to 180°C and flash the spinach in and out just before serving.

250 g baby spinach leaves	VERJUICE BUTTER SAUCE
36 large Coffin Bay scallops	4 shallots, finely sliced
sea salt	250 ml verjuice
zest and juice of 1 lime	sea salt
4 tablespoons verjuice	1 dessertspoon cream
150 g unsalted butter	250 g unsalted butter, diced
freshly ground black pepper	freshly ground black pepper
freshly grated nutmeg	lemon juice (optional)
olive oil	

To begin making the sauce, heat the shallots and verjuice with a little salt until the liquid has reduced and is syrupy. Keep warm.

Remove the stalks from the spinach if it is not really young, then wash and dry the leaves thoroughly. Clean the scallops but do not remove the roe. Season the scallops with salt, the lime zest, lime juice and verjuice.

Melt about 30 g of the butter in a saucepan until it is nut-brown. Add the spinach, then season it with salt, pepper and nutmeg and toss until just wilted. Remove the spinach to drain on kitchen paper and cover with a lid to keep warm.

Melt the remaining butter in 2 large or 3 average frying pans (it is important that the scallops are not crowded otherwise they'll poach rather than sear). When the butter has turned nut-brown, add a splash of olive oil to inhibit burning. Sear the scallops for a minute a side, then remove the pans from the heat.

Reheat the reduced verjuice and shallot mixture and add the cream. Whisk the diced butter into the reduction without allowing the sauce to boil. Season with salt and pepper and adjust with a little lemon juice, if necessary. (Strain the shallots from the sauce, if desired.)

To serve, put some spinach into the centre of 6 plates. Pile 6 scallops onto each mound of spinach, then surround with the verjuice butter sauce. Serve immediately.

SERVES 6

CARP IN VERJUICE

Soak carp caught in summer in verjuice overnight: it releases the muddy flavour and dissolves any tiny bones. Cook the fish as desired, or make a raw fish salad (ceviche).

SCALLOPS WITH

SEA-URCHIN BUTTER

These scallops are great served with drinks or as an entrée. You can either buy sea urchins from select fishmongers and collect the roe yourself, or I believe you can buy commercially produced roe from gourmet food outlets or Japanese food stores but have never tasted it. Somehow I doubt that the sweet and iron-y yet nutty intensity of the fresh roe could be bettered. It's an acquired taste, but, boy, have I acquired it.

24 Port Lincoln scallops (or fewer,
    if large), on the shell
grated zest of 1 lime
extra-virgin olive oil
sea salt
freshly ground black pepper
100 g unsalted butter
100 ml verjuice
1 handful freshly chopped chervil

SEA-URCHIN BUTTER
roe from 2 sea urchins *or* about
    2 tablespoons harvested
    sea-urchin roe
75 g softened unsalted butter
1 tablespoon lemon juice
sea salt
freshly ground black pepper

Make the sea-urchin butter by combining all the ingredients, then roll into a log, cover with plastic film and refrigerate.

Preheat the oven to 220°C or a griller until hot. Clean the scallops by pulling the meat away from the shell and cutting out the black intestinal tract. Scrub the shells and reserve them. Toss the scallops in a bowl with the lime zest, a drizzle of olive oil and some salt and pepper.

Melt the butter with 50 ml olive oil until nut-brown, then pan-fry the scallops in batches for about 30 seconds each side, just to seal them (don't try to cook too many scallops at once – you want to sear

not poach them). Add the verjuice to the pan to deglaze it.

Return a scallop to each half-shell, then dot with a slice of sea-urchin butter and drizzle with the verjuice pan juices. Put the scallops on their shells into the oven or under the griller for about a minute, just until the butter begins to melt. Sprinkle with chervil and serve immediately.

MAKES 24

PAN-FRIED CARP

Although many people don't believe me, I love to cook carp – but only when it's young, fresh and pink (having been caught when the waters of the Murray are cold) and when it's filleted well. Dust the fillets in seasoned flour, then pan-fry them in nut-brown butter for about 2 minutes a side and deglaze the pan with verjuice. Top with a slice of anchovy butter before serving, if you like.

SALMON IN VERJUICE

FOR A PARTY

This is my interpretation of a dish described to me in December 1999 by a customer at our farm shop. A caterer had prepared something similar for a Christmas function, and her guests had been so delighted with it they had all asked for more. This conversation in mind, I put the following together, although I reduced the verjuice rather than just bringing it to a boil, which was the way it was described to me. I am only sorry I didn't get the customer's name so I could acknowledge her generosity.

2 sides skinned Atlantic salmon *or*
    ocean trout, off the bone
2 tablespoons sea salt
1 cup freshly plucked chervil leaves
750 ml verjuice
250 ml extra-virgin olive oil
    (optional)

Remove the pin bones from the salmon, then cut each side into thin fillets in the same way smoked salmon is prepared. Re-form the original shape. Carefully transfer each side to a rectangular, heat-resistant glass dish and lie one on top of the other, adding a little salt and chervil as you go.

Reduce the verjuice over heat by almost half and pour it gently over the salmon to just cover it, then cover securely with a lid. (I add olive oil to the reduced verjuice for a more robust flavour.) Our visitor told us that by the time the guests had come to the table the heat of the verjuice had cooked the salmon.

Serve with buttery boiled new potatoes.

SERVES 20

VERJUICE-MARINATED SASHIMI

Next time you are holidaying by the beach and have caught your own fish, or have access to a supplier with super-fresh produce, consider making sashimi with verjuice. Any firm, white-fleshed fish can be used (snapper, gar, coral trout, flathead and whiting work well), as can salmon or ocean trout. Just remember: if the flesh isn't top-notch, don't bother! To make enough dressing for 2 whiting fillets, which will serve 4–6 people as an entrée or a pre-dinner snack, bring 125 ml verjuice and 2 chopped shallots to a boil in a non-reactive saucepan and reduce by half. Remove from the heat and allow to cool, then add 2 tablespoons freshly plucked chervil and 3 tablespoons extra-virgin olive oil and season. Put 2 skinned fish fillets into a deep glass dish and pour over the dressing. Marinate for 30 minutes, then slice and serve with lemon wedges alongside.

MORETON BAY BUGS WOK-SEARED WITH CITRUS AND VERJUICE ON CRUSTACEAN BLINI

This recipe, from former restaurant The Duck in Melbourne's casino complex on the banks of the Yarra, first appeared in a collection put together by Garry Crittenden of Dromana Estate winery.

250 ml verjuice

200 ml fish stock

50 g unsalted butter, diced

40 g finely diced grapefruit, lemon and orange

vegetable oil

2 cloves garlic, crushed

4 shallots, finely diced

250 g Moreton Bay bug meat

good-quality tangerine oil

BLINI

4 eggs

2 tablespoons milk

salt

freshly ground black pepper

80 g plain flour, sifted

30 g crayfish

30 g crabmeat

freshly chopped chives

Reduce the verjuice over heat by two-thirds, then add the fish stock and reduce by half. Remove from the heat and whisk in the butter. Add the diced citrus and bring to a simmer, then set aside.

Heat a wok or frying pan and add a little vegetable oil. Sauté the garlic and shallots until soft but not coloured, then add the bug meat and sauté until just cooked. Set aside and keep warm.

Preheat the oven to 90°C. To make the blini, whisk the eggs, milk and seasonings together, then fold in the flour followed by the crayfish, crabmeat and chives. Cook a tablespoon of this mixture at a time in a hot, non-stick frying pan until golden brown, then flip the blini over to cook the other side. Repeat the process with the remaining batter, keeping the cooked blini warm in the oven as you do so.

To serve, put the bug meat into the citrus sauce and warm through while the blini warm in the oven. Put 2 blini on each plate, then, using tongs, put a little bug meat on each blini. Spoon the sauce gently over each serve, then garnish with a little freshly ground black pepper and a very small drizzle of tangerine oil. Serve immediately.

SERVES 4

OCEAN TROUT CEVICHE

For an effortless luncheon that you can make the night before, dust fillets of the freshest ocean trout in seasoned flour, with fresh tarragon or chervil if it is available, then gently fry in butter over a medium heat to seal the surface on both sides. Put in a flat serving dish and then prepare the marinade. Reduce 250 ml verjuice by half with 2 finely chopped shallots, take off the heat and quickly add 125 ml extra-virgin olive oil, some fresh chervil or tarragon, sea salt and pepper. Immediately pour over the warm fish, which will be rosy in the centre but 'cooked' by the marinade. Cover and refrigerate for a couple of hours. Take from the refrigerator 2 hours before serving. If you feel like really spoiling yourself, purée a tongue or two of sea-urchin roe into the marinade. Alternatively, serve the ceviche with salmon roe scattered on top.

SKATE WITH CAPERS
AND OLIVES

I adapted the following recipe from Ann and Franco Taruschio's Leaves
from the Walnut Tree, *a favourite book. Skate, the wings of a stingray,
is inexpensive. In some states it is sold untrimmed with the skin on, so
you may need to clean it; better still, ask the fishmonger to do it for you.*

4 × 225 g pieces of skate

sea salt

freshly ground black pepper

plain flour

2 cloves garlic

extra-virgin olive oil

1 handful flat-leaf parsley

12 black olives

4 tablespoons capers

4 tablespoons verjuice

squeeze of lemon juice

Preheat the oven to 180°C and trim
the skate of skin if this has not
already been done. Season the flour.
Finely chop the garlic and brown it
in 4 tablespoons olive oil in a large,
ovenproof, heavy-based frying pan,
being careful not to burn it.

Dust each piece of the skate with
the seasoned flour and brown it
in the pan with the garlic for about
2 minutes a side, depending on the
thickness.

Remove the stems from the
parsley and reserve them, then
chop the leaves (you need about
2 tablespoons chopped parsley).
Stone and slice the olives. Add the

parsley stems with the olives, capers, verjuice and lemon juice to the skate, then season.

Transfer the pan to the oven and bake for 4 minutes, then turn the skate over and bake for another 2 minutes. Toss the skate with the chopped parsley on a warmed serving platter, then drizzle on a little extra-virgin olive oil. Reduce the sauce in the pan over heat and pour over the skate. Serve with boiled waxy potatoes.

SERVES 4

WARM OLIVE AND HERB VINAIGRETTE
Make a warm vinaigrette with pipped olives, capers, oregano, flat-leaf parsley, verjuice and extra-virgin olive oil to use with a thick fish fillet, such as snapper. Dust the fillets with seasoned flour and pan-fry or bake until just opaque. Pour the warm vinaigrette over and serve immediately. Just as good with pan-fried chicken breasts.

TUNA ROLLS WITH CURRANTS, PINE NUTS AND BAY LEAVES

This recipe is based on one in Mary Taylor Simeti's wonderful book Pomp and Sustenance. *My method differs, and I use tuna rather than swordfish. I prefer to choose whichever tuna is in season: yellowfin or bluefin. If you cannot buy tuna trimmed of its skin and bloodline, allow an extra 150 g to ensure you end up with 1 kg trimmed weight. Marlin is also suitable for this dish.*

1 × 1 kg piece trimmed tuna
1 large red onion
32 fresh bay leaves
extra-virgin olive oil
lemon wedges

FILLING
¼ cup currants
2 tablespoons verjuice
¼ cup pine nuts
1–2 tablespoons extra-virgin olive oil
1 cup flat-leaf parsley
5 cloves garlic
sea salt
freshly ground black pepper
120 g freshly grated pecorino

To begin making the filling, soak the currants in the verjuice overnight or on low in a microwave oven for 5 minutes.

Preheat the oven to 230°C. Soak 16 bamboo skewers in water for 30 minutes to prevent them burning during cooking.

Moisten the pine nuts with a little of the olive oil and roast on a baking tray in the oven for about 5 minutes until golden brown. Keep an eye on them as they burn easily. Chop the parsley and garlic together well, then add the pine nuts and the drained currants and chop roughly. Season to taste and thoroughly stir in the pecorino and 1 tablespoon olive oil.

Keep the tuna chilled until you are ready to use it. If not already trimmed, strip away the skin just as you would a fillet of beef and then cut out the bloodline. Cut the tuna into 24 thin slices about 10 cm × 7.5 cm and about 3 mm thick. Gently flatten any smaller slices by putting each between two pieces of plastic film and gently tapping it with a soft mallet as if it were a scaloppine.

Peel and quarter the onion, then separate it into crescents. Place a teaspoon of the currant filling on one end of each slice of tuna and roll it up as neatly as possible, then spear on a skewer with a piece of onion. Follow with a bay leaf, then another roll of tuna, then onion, and so on until 8 of the skewers have been filled

(3 rolls and 4 bay leaves per skewer). Run a second skewer through the rolls parallel to the first skewer but a couple of centimetres apart and repeat with the remaining skewers. Make sure the skewers aren't packed too tightly: it is important that the tuna parcels don't touch, otherwise the fish will stew rather than grill or roast.

If grilling the rolls, heat the griller as high as it can go, otherwise roast at 250°C. Brush the filled skewers with olive oil and grill for 2 minutes on the first side and 1 minute on the second, or roast for 5 minutes just to seal one side. The tuna should be only just seared and the onion needs to be nothing more than warm.

Serve with extra-virgin olive oil and lemon wedges. Any leftovers are delectable the next day, when the flavours have had time to meld.

SERVES 8

CARPACCIO OF WILD BARRAMUNDI
WITH VERJUICE AND RED GRAPES

This recipe, from the famed but sadly defunct Melbourne restaurant Marchetti's Latin, first appeared in a collection put together by Garry Crittenden of Dromana Estate winery.

750 ml verjuice
50 ml pomegranate molasses
100 g red grapes
600 g wild barramundi fillet
extra-virgin olive oil
sea salt
freshly ground black pepper
sprigs of chervil

Reduce the verjuice by half over heat, then allow to cool. Add the pomegranate molasses and grapes to the cooled verjuice reduction and marinate for at least 2 hours.

Just before serving, slice the barramundi as thinly as possible and arrange the slices in a circle on a plate. Drizzle with the verjuice reduction and extra-virgin olive oil to cover, then scatter over the grapes. Finish the dish with a sprinkling of salt and pepper and the chervil.

SERVES 8

Tetsuya Wakuda, of Tetsuya's in Sydney, cooks like a dream, pays amazing attention to detail and is one of the most generous, delightful souls I have met. His Japanese-inspired cooking has won him several awards, including the Remy Martin Cognac/Australian Gourmet Traveller Restaurant of the Year award in 1993 and 1996, GT's first-ever Award for Excellence in 1999, and the Sydney Morning Herald Award for Professional Excellence in 2002.

I think of verjuice as another kind of vinegar, and use it instead of rice-wine vinegar at times. The flavour isn't so strong it spoils the flavour of the food: as an acidulant it is almost unnoticeable. The acid is not at the front of the palate as it is sometimes with vinegar.

I use verjuice in a vinaigrette with kelp as a sauce for fish, or I reconstitute kelp in it. I also use verjuice in a dish with barramundi and bitter greens, and when poaching fish, especially muddy fish. It is good, too, with sardines – it takes away the 'fishy' flavour. I also sometimes make sushi rice with it. Verjuice is lovely with peaches, which I marinate in it.

TETSUYA WAKUDA

OYSTERS WITH LEEKS AND VERJUICE

Until April 2000, Hungarian-born George Biron and his partner, Diane Garrett, ran Sunnybrae, an extraordinary restaurant in the hills behind Lorne on Victoria's west coast. The menus were always seasonally driven, and a walk to the impressive kitchen garden midway through lunch in the sunny dining room was just about compulsory. I spent a very happy weekend at Sunnybrae teaching at a cooking school with Stephanie Alexander. The light streaming into the kitchen and the outlook onto the garden made it the most enjoyable commercial environment in which I have ever worked.

George comments, 'This recipe celebrates the original intentions of the nouvelle cuisine movement of the 1970s (not the bad copyists). All it takes are small leeks (so underrated), freshly opened oysters and an old ingredient, verjuice.'

18 tiny leeks
500 ml verjuice
30 freshly opened oysters
1 tablespoon dried wakame seaweed
sea salt
freshly ground black pepper

Poach the leeks in the verjuice until tender. Remove the leeks, then set them aside in a little of the poaching liquid. Add the liquor from the oysters to the remaining verjuice and reduce by half over heat. Add the oysters and wakame to the reduced verjuice to warm through. Season and serve with good sourdough rye bread.

SERVES 6

WARM SALAD OF RED FIN

This recipe comes from Stefano de Pieri's wonderful book, A Gondola on the Murray *(volume 1), which accompanied the television series of the same name.*

1 × 600 g red fin
mixed green salad leaves
light olive oil
sea salt
verjuice

Red fin has a tough skin. If you cook it with the skin on, this forms a natural heat chamber in which the flesh will cook neatly. So cook the fish on a tray in the oven at 180°C for 10–15 minutes. Then remove the skin at once and take the flesh from the bone. Do it quickly, then put the meat over tender green leaves and dress at once with a dressing made with a light olive oil, salt and verjuice.

SERVES 2–3

MARINATED YABBIES IN VINE LEAVES

Marinate cooked yabbies or prawns in extra-virgin olive oil and a dash of verjuice and wrap in tender vine leaves blanched in verjuice. Cook in a hot oven for a few minutes dotted with a little butter and seasoned with salt and pepper.

STUFFED TROUT WITH VERJUICE SAUCE

I met Chef Pierre Corre of Auberge du Truffe in Périgueux when I was travelling with Stephanie Alexander in France in November 1999. The Master of the local truffle market had taken us to lunch, and Pierre made us the most extravagant omelette laden with a huge truffle fresh from that morning's market, the first of the season. The shame of it was that I didn't know of Pierre's interest in reviving the verjuice tradition until we were leaving France. I came across a magazine article that Stephanie translated for me as we flew home – it was only then that I realised the opportunity I'd missed. I contacted Chef Pierre on arriving home to confirm his interest and to ask for a contribution to this book: I was happy to receive an affirmative response on both counts.

While this recipe uses stock made from the bones of a smoked fish, ordinary fish stock can be used too. If making a smoked stock, do so with great discretion: it can end up being very salty and overpowering if you are not careful.

6 × 250 g trout	VERJUICE SAUCE
softened butter	250 ml smoked fish stock
sea salt	250 ml dry white wine
freshly ground black pepper	200 g shallots, chopped
freshly chopped flat-leaf parsley	125 ml verjuice
green grapes	200–250 g unsalted butter
	sea salt
	freshly ground black pepper

STUFFING

350 g bread

dry white wine

1 shallot, finely chopped

3 cloves garlic, finely chopped

a few flat-leaf parsley sprigs

100 g fresh cèpes or porcini *or*

    10 g dried porcini, reconstituted

    and drained

1 egg

To prepare the trout, cut away the fins and scale the fish. Remove the guts through the gills (not through the belly), then wash and dry the fish well. (You could also ask your fishmonger to prepare it for you.)

To make the sauce, put the stock, wine and shallots into a stainless steel or enamelled saucepan and cook until the shallots have softened and the liquid has reduced. Blend this mixture in a food processor, then add the verjuice. Return to the pan and stir in the butter, a knob at a time, then season. Set aside.

To make the stuffing, soak the bread in a little wine, then squeeze out any excess moisture. Mix the bread with the shallot, garlic, parsley and mushrooms and season. Add the egg to bind the mixture together. Using a piping bag, fill each fish with the stuffing through the gills.

Preheat the oven to 200°C. Smear a baking dish or sheet of foil with butter. Put the fish into the dish, then season and dot with a little more butter.

Cook the fish, uncovered, in the oven for 10 minutes, then turn it over carefully. Cook for another 6–8 minutes.

To serve, warm the sauce gently. Arrange the stuffed trout on a plate, then cover with the sauce. Sprinkle with chopped parsley and grapes.

SERVES 6

OCEAN TROUT IN VERJUICE JELLY

This entrée is beautiful – it sparkles on the plate and palate, and is best when the ingredients are first-rate. I first made it using Murray cod for a wine dinner for 400 people. I wanted something very fresh to serve as an entrée with rhine riesling. Murray cod worked wonderfully, but is hard to obtain. If ocean trout isn't available, try fresh salmon instead.

unsalted butter
3–4 sage leaves
extra-virgin olive oil
1 tablespoon minced fennel
1 teaspoon grated lemongrass
1 tablespoon freshly chopped
    flat-leaf parsley
1 generous handful chervil
sea salt
freshly ground black pepper
1 × 1.5 kg premium-quality
    ocean trout *or* yellowtail
    kingfish
4 shallots, chopped
2 sprigs rosemary
2 bay leaves
5½ leaves gelatine
400 ml verjuice

Melt a knob of butter in a frying pan and cook until nut-brown, then crisp the sage leaves in the butter and drain on paper towel. Wipe out the pan and add a little extra-virgin olive oil. Sauté the fennel and lemongrass in the oil, then add the parsley and 1 tablespoon chopped chervil off the heat (this preserves the colour and flavour of the herbs). Season with salt and pepper and set aside to cool.

Preheat the oven to 150°C, then gut the fish. Tumble the shallots, rosemary, bay leaves and remaining chervil together in a baking dish or fish kettle large enough to take the fish comfortably. Open the fish out and position it on the shallot mixture, belly-side down, then drizzle it with olive oil and season with salt and pepper. Cover the baking dish with foil and cook for about 15 minutes (the foil will ensure the fish steams and cooks quickly). Remove the fish from the oven and put it aside to 'set'. (You can do this in the refrigerator, but don't let the fish cool completely or the fillets will be difficult to remove intact.) Once the fish has firmed up, discard the skin and carefully remove the fillets.

Soak the gelatine in a little cold water for 5 minutes. Meanwhile, warm the verjuice in a non-reactive saucepan (don't allow it to boil, though, or it will become cloudy). Remove the softened gelatine sheets from the water and squeeze out the excess moisture before dropping them into the warm verjuice. Stir gently over low heat until the gelatine has dissolved. Set aside to cool a little.

Pour some of the cooled jelly mixture into a 1-litre mould large enough to accommodate the fish fillets, remembering that the tail ends will be doubled over to ensure even thickness. The jelly layer should be as deep as the fillets are at their thickest point. Cover the mould with plastic wrap and refrigerate until set – this will take at least an hour, depending on your refrigerator (it's best to do it well in advance). Arrange a layer of fish over the jelly, doubling the tail ends over to maintain an even thickness, then top this with the crisped sage leaves and the fennel mixture. Pour in another jelly layer, then refrigerate until set as before (if the jelly has firmed up too much to pour, warm it a little over low heat).

To serve, dip the base of the mould in hot water and quickly invert the jelly onto a plate. To have the herb-side uppermost, invert the jelly onto another plate. Cut into 4 portions using a hot knife and serve immediately.

SERVES 4

Poultry

BAROSSA CHOOK AND PICKLED CUMQUAT TERRINE

CORN-FED CHICKEN WITH POTATOES AND BAY LEAVES

CHICKEN BREASTS WITH ROSEMARY, PINE NUTS AND VERJUICE

BONED CHICKEN STUFFED WITH GIBLETS AND PROSCIUTTO

GRAPEGROWER'S CHICKEN

CHICKEN IN THE OVEN WITH VERJUICE

SALAD OF GRILLED QUAIL WITH LEMON VINAIGRETTE

QUAIL ROASTED WITH CUMQUATS AND VERJUICE

PHEASANT WITH SULTANA GRAPES AND VERJUICE

PARTRIDGE WITH SAVOY CABBAGE AND PANCETTA

ROAST DUCK WITH VERJUICE SAUCE

ROAST DUCK WITH LIVER AND WALNUT STUFFING

SALAD OF DUCK LIVER, APPLE, WALNUTS AND CARAMELISED GARLIC

BAROSSA CHOOK AND
PICKLED CUMQUAT TERRINE

I'm lucky to have first-rate free-range chooks almost literally on my doorstep. An interest in food runs in the family – my eldest daughter, Saskia, and her husband, Greg, are responsible for producing corn-fed, free-range, chemical- and hormone-free chickens under the Barossa Chooks label, part of their Barossa Farm Produce range.

Dried green peppercorns can be used here, too, as long as the terrine is eaten the day after it's cooked.

2 tablespoons green peppercorns
375 ml verjuice
1 × 2.25 kg Barossa Chook
275 ml extra-virgin olive oil
12 fresh bay leaves
1 cup firmly packed basil leaves
1 cup seeded and chopped Pickled
    Cumquats (see page 22)
1 tablespoon freshly chopped
    tarragon
1 tablespoon salt

Soak the peppercorns in a little of the verjuice at least overnight to rid them of any briny flavour (the peppercorns can, in fact, be stored indefinitely like this).

Bone the chook, keeping the skin as intact as possible. Set the skin aside, then cut the breasts into 4 strips, the legs into 3 and the thighs into 4 and transfer to a ceramic or glass dish. Combine the soaked peppercorns with the remaining ingredients, except the salt, then pour this over the chicken. Cover well with plastic film and refrigerate for 24 hours.

Preheat the oven to 160°C. Line a terrine with the reserved chicken skin, making sure that any excess is allowed to hang over the rim. Pack the chicken, peppercorns, herbs, cumquats and salt into the terrine, then seal neatly with the chicken skin. Stand the terrine in a baking dish and pour in water to come two-thirds of the way up the sides of the mould. Cook for 2½ hours, then remove from the oven.

Weight the terrine as it cools – it can be left for several days this way in the refrigerator. Cut into slices and serve with a fresh rocket salad and pickled watermelon rind.

SERVES 8

POT-ROASTED CHICKEN

Brown a chicken in goose fat, olive oil or butter in a large casserole, then add garlic cloves, a sprig of rosemary, 125 ml chicken stock and 125 ml verjuice and pot-roast for 40–60 minutes. Turn the chook occasionally and add more verjuice or stock as necessary. A delicious syrupy glaze will develop around the bird.

CORN-FED CHICKEN WITH

POTATOES AND BAY LEAVES

This recipe comes from Stephanie Alexander. When planning our cooking classes in Tuscany in 1997, Stephanie suggested we take verjuice with us. We used it in everything from pasta dishes and savoury sauces to desserts, and were only limited by our imagination.

We found the roasting chickens in Italy absolutely delicious – the Italians are very awake to the benefits of truly free-ranged birds. These were deep-breasted, yellow-fleshed, full-flavoured and tender chickens. Look for the very best free-range bird you can afford and serve chicken as a treat.

2 × 1.8 kg corn-fed free-range
   chickens

1 lemon, cut into 4 thick slices

2 fresh bay leaves

3 tablespoons extra-virgin olive oil

sea salt

freshly ground black pepper

6 large potatoes, quartered

12 large cloves garlic, unpeeled

2 tablespoons verjuice

250 ml chicken stock

Preheat the oven to 220°C. Cut up either side of the backbone of each chicken to remove it, then remove the wishbone, leaving the extra skin at the neck edge. Loosen the skin over the breast and work a slice of lemon and half a bay leaf under the skin over each breast. Smooth the skin back into place and wipe the chicken dry. Rub 2 tablespoons of the oil seasoned with salt and pepper over each bird.

Dry the potatoes and roll them in the remaining oil with the unpeeled garlic cloves. Scatter the potatoes and garlic over the base of a large baking dish. Open out the chickens and settle them skin-side up over the potatoes, then roast for 40 minutes.

Remove the dish from the oven and loosen the potatoes and garlic. Reduce the temperature to 200°C and return the dish to the oven for a further 15 minutes. The chicken is done if the juices run clear when a thigh is pierced with a fine skewer. Remove the chicken to a heated platter and cover loosely with foil. (Crisp the potatoes on a fresh baking dish if required.)

Stand the baking dish over heat and allow the juices to bubble hard, scraping any crispy and caramelised bits from the bottom. Add the verjuice and stock and boil until you have a well-flavoured sauce. Joint the chickens and return them to the platter with the potatoes and garlic. Check the seasoning of the sauce and spoon over the chicken.

SERVES 8

PAN-FRIED CHICKEN BREASTS

Cook seasoned chicken breasts or legs, skin-side down, in nut-brown butter until well coloured, then turn until just cooked through. Drain off any excess butter and deglaze the pan with verjuice. This technique will turn even a supermarket chook into a really tasty dish.

CHICKEN BREASTS WITH
ROSEMARY, PINE NUTS
AND VERJUICE

This dish came about when I was asked to cook something simple at our Farm Shop for a television show that was to screen in the United States. As commercial kitchens are pretty sterile places, I decided to use a portable hot plate in the wintergarden at the shop instead, giving me the chance to show the American viewers just what a beautiful spot we have. I had to use as little equipment as possible and had just minutes to pull the dish together – it was a bit like cooking on holidays! But what a deliciously easy and fresh result . . .

⅓ cup raisins

100 ml verjuice

2 sprigs rosemary

extra-virgin olive oil

freshly ground black pepper

4 chicken breasts, skin on

⅓ cup pine nuts

20 g butter

sea salt

Soak the raisins overnight in the verjuice. (Alternatively, microwave the raisins and verjuice on the defrost setting for about 5 minutes, then allow to cool.) Strain, reserving the verjuice.

Strip the rosemary leaves from the stalks and reserve the leaves for another use. Put the stalks into a bowl with 3 tablespoons olive oil and a little pepper. Add the chicken breasts and marinate for at least 1 hour.

Choose a wide frying pan with enough room for the chicken breasts to cook with lots of space between them. (If you don't have a pan big enough, you'll have to do them in batches.) Toss the pine nuts with a little olive oil over medium heat in this pan until golden brown. Keep an eye on them as they burn easily. Tip the pine nuts out onto paper towel to cool.

Cook the butter in the frying pan until golden brown, then add 1 tablespoon olive oil to inhibit burning. Pan-fry the chicken over moderate heat, skin-side down, until well sealed and golden, 6–10 minutes. Turn and cook the other side for 3–4 minutes.

(The total cooking time will depend on the thickness of the breasts, but as a rule, two-thirds of the cooking time should be done on the skin side.)

When the chicken breasts are cooked through, season them and remove from the pan. Rest in a warm place, skin-side down. Discard any butter left in the pan and toss in the raisins. Pour in the reserved verjuice and deglaze the pan over heat until the liquid has reduced by half, then stir in the pine nuts. Pour the sauce over the chicken and serve with soft polenta, or potatoes mashed with olive oil.

SERVES 4

BARBECUED QUAIL OR CHICKEN
Plunge quail or chicken straight from grilling on the barbecue into a 'bath' of verjuice, fresh herbs and extra-virgin olive oil and rest before serving.

BONED CHICKEN STUFFED WITH GIBLETS AND PROSCIUTTO

Verjuice added to a sauce or poaching stock, as in this recipe, provides a really identifiable freshness. If the poaching liquid is then reduced, the verjuice enhances the viscosity of the final sauce, ensuring it becomes unctuous and syrupy.

125 ml verjuice
4 litres jellied chicken stock
1 × 1.6 kg boned corn-fed
   free-range chicken
sea salt

STUFFING
100 g chicken giblets
100 g chicken hearts
unsalted butter
2 tablespoons freshly chopped
   herbs (preferably rosemary
   and marjoram)
freshly ground black pepper
1 large onion
2 cups coarse stale breadcrumbs
extra-virgin olive oil
200 g finely sliced prosciutto
1 teaspoon Dijon mustard

Preheat the oven to 230°C. To make the stuffing, cook the giblets and hearts in a saucepan in a little butter with the herbs and a grinding of pepper, then chop finely and set aside. Chop the onion roughly and sweat it until soft in butter over gentle heat in the wiped-out pan, then add it to the giblet mixture. Toss the breadcrumbs with a little olive oil and toast in the oven until golden, watching that they don't burn. Chop the prosciutto finely and add with the mustard and breadcrumbs to the giblet mixture.

Reduce the verjuice by half over high heat. Warm the reduced

84

verjuice and stock in a saucepan big enough to take the stuffed chicken later on.

Flatten out the boned bird and spread it with the stuffing, then roll it up and wrap it in muslin. Put the stuffed bird into the stock – it is important that at least three-quarters of the bird is immersed. Poach for 20 minutes at a very gentle simmer,

then turn the bird over and poach for another 20 minutes. Remove the chicken and wrap it in foil to rest for 30 minutes.

Reduce the poaching liquid to a sauce. Slice the chicken and serve it with the sauce and a dollop of Salsa Agresto (see pages 14–15).

SERVES 6

PAN-FRIED CHICKEN LIVERS WITH CURRANTS
Pan-fry chicken or duck livers in nut-brown butter. At the last minute toss in currants or sultanas soaked in verjuice and deglaze the pan with the soaking juices.

GRAPEGROWER'S CHICKEN

Here the recipe includes instructions for making fresh verjuice, although you can easily substitute the bought variety. If you wish to make this dish when grapes are out of season, use commercial verjuice and, instead of adding grapes to the sauce, in the last 5 minutes of cooking add ½ cup raisins soaked overnight in medium–dry sherry.

1 kg unripe sultana grapes
4 large corn-fed free-range chicken
    legs (thighs and drumsticks)
walnut oil
unsalted butter
sea salt
freshly ground black pepper
125 ml jellied chicken stock
1 cup ripe sultana grapes

Make the verjuice by blending the unripe grapes in a food processor, then strain and set aside (you need 160 ml).

Separate the thighs and drumsticks. Heat enough oil and 1 tablespoon butter to just cover the bottom of a heavy-based casserole and gently seal the chicken pieces until golden brown.

Season the chicken with salt and pepper and discard the oil in the pan. Add the verjuice and gently braise the chicken. Be careful that the temperature is not so high that the skin sticks and the verjuice caramelises – if this starts to happen, add a little stock or water.

Cook for about 20 minutes until tender, then set aside, covered, for about 10 minutes.

Add the stock to the pan and reduce over heat. While the sauce is boiling rapidly, whisk in 100 g diced, chilled butter to 'velvet' the sauce. Throw in the ripe grapes in the last few seconds of cooking. Serve the chicken with the sauce, a green salad and boiled waxy potatoes.

SERVES 6

DUCK, GOOSE OR CHOOK LIVERS
In countries where duck or goose foie gras is available, verjuice added to the pan-fried liver provides the perfect balance to the richness. In Australia, fresh blond livers from mature free-range chooks will have to suffice.

CHICKEN IN THE OVEN
WITH VERJUICE

This recipe comes from Stefano de Pieri's book, A Gondola on the Murray *(volume 1).*

4 cloves garlic
1 large knob ginger
1 chilli
**1 × 1.5 kg free-range chicken, boned
and cut in half**
sea salt
freshly ground black pepper
olive oil
3 tablespoons verjuice
3 tablespoons cream
1 knob butter
basil or coriander

Preheat the oven to 180°C. Finely chop the garlic, ginger and chilli. Put the chopped aromatics between each chicken breast and thigh and fold like a sandwich. Season with salt and pepper. In a cast-iron pan, brown both sides of the chicken in hot olive oil and then transfer to the oven. Roast for 15 minutes until still a little pink inside.

Rest the chicken, covered, in a warm place for at least 10 minutes. Add the verjuice to the pan and reduce over high heat, then add the cream and reduce again. Add the butter to the sauce away from the heat to make a smooth sauce.

Cut each piece of chicken into four and dress with the sauce. Sprinkle with basil or coriander and serve with roasted potatoes and a green salad.

SERVES 4

There can't be anyone in Australia who doesn't know of Stephanie Alexander and her incredible influence on our culinary scene. She is a chef, award-winning restaurateur, television presenter and food writer of great note, and I'm lucky enough to count her as a great friend and travelling companion, as well as an inspiration.

When I made my first-ever batch of verjuice in 1984, I shared some flagons around. Stephanie was the first person to ask for more. It was also Stephanie who convinced me to take verjuice with us to Tuscany when we ran cooking schools there. (We used it so regularly that we had to ask Colin to bring more with him when he flew over to join us for the last school and our holiday together!) Stephanie's support and encouragement have been unflagging, and for that I am truly grateful.

I like to use verjuice rather than vinegar when braising ingredients, particularly fennel. Best of all, I love a bit of verjuice to deglaze a pan when cooking chicken, especially when roasting a whole bird with small onions and potatoes. After the chicken has been removed from the pan and set aside to rest, drained of any juices in the cavity, I deglaze the baking dish with verjuice to make a simple sauce.

STEPHANIE ALEXANDER

SALAD OF GRILLED QUAIL, ROAST PARSNIP, HAZELNUTS AND VERJUICE WITH LEMON VINAIGRETTE

This recipe comes from Philip Johnson, owner–chef of the highly successful e'cco bistro in Brisbane, which won the Remy Martin Cognac/Australian Gourmet Traveller Restaurant of the Year award in 1997. The simplicity of Philip's cooking, in which he lets each ingredient shine through, makes eating at e'cco a delight, and a 'must' whenever I'm in Brisbane.

6 parsnips, peeled, halved and cored

few sprigs of thyme

5 cloves garlic, unpeeled and lightly crushed

olive oil

6 large quail, boned

sea salt

freshly ground black pepper

VINAIGRETTE

100 ml verjuice

juice of 1 lemon

2 teaspoons grainy mustard

1 tablespoon freshly chopped thyme

150 ml vegetable oil

150 ml extra-virgin oil

sea salt

freshly ground black pepper

SALAD

2 witlof bulbs, leaves separated

100 g curly endive *or* rocket, washed

½ red onion, finely sliced

½ cup flat-leaf parsley leaves

1 cup roughly chopped roasted hazelnuts

Preheat the oven to 180°C. Mix the parsnips, thyme and garlic with a little olive oil in a bowl until well coated. Put the parsnips onto a baking tray and roast until tender, then set aside. Increase the oven temperature to 200°C.

Heat a heavy-based ovenproof frying pan over high heat. Brush

90

the quail with olive oil, then season with salt and pepper. Put the quail skin-side down in the pan and sear until a good colour is achieved. Turn the quail over and put the pan in the oven and roast for 4–5 minutes. Remove the quail and allow to rest while assembling the salad.

To make the vinaigrette, put the verjuice, lemon juice, mustard and thyme into a bowl. Whisk in the combined oils, then season to taste with salt and pepper. Just before serving, mix the salad ingredients in a large bowl and dress with just enough vinaigrette to moisten the leaves.

To serve, quarter the warm quail and gently reheat the parsnip. Arrange some parsnip on each plate and put a quail breast and 2 legs on top. Divide the salad between the plates. Finish by putting the remaining quail breasts on top of each salad. Drizzle the remaining vinaigrette on and around the salad.

SERVES 6

SAUCE FOR ROASTED GAME BIRDS

Roast garlic in the oven until golden and soft, then add pancetta and sage to crisp. Remove the pan from the oven and toss in fresh grapes, then deglaze with verjuice over heat for a sauce to serve with roasted game birds.

Tony Tan, the effervescent chef, food writer, television presenter and culinary tour leader, finds many uses for verjuice in his Asian-dominated approach to food. Tony has been a friend since we shared a meal at our kitchen table in the Barossa when he was helping to plan the SBS Food Lovers' Guide to Australia *television series.*

Verjuice goes very well with my Chinese-style roast chicken. I marinate the bird in five-spice, honey, light soy, sometimes rice wine and verjuice – it sits in the fridge for a couple of hours. I roast the bird in the usual manner and finish the sauce with either a splash of extra verjuice or stock. Some sliced cucumber is my preferred accompaniment.

Sometimes I mix verjuice with fish stock and a touch of light soy, add pickled Chinese limes and pour this over fillets of snapper or bream. The fillets are then quickly steamed and are fabulous. Naturally, the inspiration is Chinese, and the verjuice provides perfect sour flavours without masking the delicacy of the fish.

Although pork or chicken adobo was originally a Spanish dish, the Filipino version is nothing like what is offered on the Iberian peninsula. In the Philippines, soy sauce and vinegar are added along with water to garlic, black pepper, bay leaves and the meat of your choice. The dish is cooked until the meat is tender and the sauce reduced. I add verjuice, about half a cup, just when the sauce is becoming syrupy. Verjuice is less harsh than vinegar and with a splash of lime juice the adobo, although still not traditional, is simply delicious.

TONY TAN

QUAIL ROASTED WITH
CUMQUATS AND VERJUICE

A quick and delicious meal – in less than half an hour! You can also use chicken thigh meat, a much-neglected cut, instead of quail: you will need to cook 4 large chicken thighs at 180°C for 25 minutes until golden.

12 nagami cumquats

8 quail

unsalted butter

extra-virgin olive oil

3 tablespoons verjuice

sea salt

freshly ground black pepper

½ cup flat-leaf parsley leaves

Preheat the oven to 230°C. Remove the stalks from the cumquats and cut the fruit in half lengthwise.

Spatchcock the quail by cutting down either side of the backbone and then discarding it. Flatten out the birds and, using your thumbs, pull the wings away from the breast and tuck them behind the body.

Heat a little butter and olive oil in a frying pan and seal the quail, skin-side down, over a high heat until caramelised. Transfer to a baking dish, skin-side up, and scatter over the cumquats. Using a pastry brush, paint the quail with 2 tablespoons of the verjuice and drizzle over a little olive oil. Season and roast for 6 minutes. Remove from the oven and pour the remaining verjuice over, then allow to rest, breast down, for 5–10 minutes.

To serve, drizzle the juices in the baking dish over the quail and cumquats, then scatter with the parsley.

SERVES 4

PHEASANT WITH SULTANA GRAPES
AND VERJUICE

This tried-and-true dish comes from the old Pheasant Farm days. The majority of our customers wanted to eat pheasant, so I can assure you I could cook them with my eyes closed. But for all our sakes I always wanted to use as many different flavours as I could. During vintage the following was our most frequently cooked dish: by this time that year's verjuice was in the bottle, the pheasants were in their natural season, and the first of the sultana grapes were being picked. A truly seasonal dish.

While this recipe includes a rich butter sauce, it works equally well if the butter is omitted from the sauce.

3 × 800 g young hen pheasants
1 lemon
sea salt
freshly ground black pepper
100 g chilled unsalted butter, diced
250 ml verjuice
250 ml reduced veal, chicken *or* game
   stock
2 cups sultana grapes

Preheat the oven to 250°C. Remove the second joint and wing tip from the pheasants, leaving only the first joint of the wing as an exposed bone. Cut through the skin around the thigh to free the legs a little, but do not remove them completely.

Squeeze a little lemon juice into the cavity of each bird and season with salt and pepper. Melt a little of the butter in a frying pan and brown the birds gently on all sides

until golden brown. Arrange the
birds in a baking dish, allowing
the legs to spread. Bake for
10–12 minutes. Remove from
the oven and turn over, then cover
and rest in a warm place for
15 minutes.

Meanwhile, deglaze the baking
dish with the verjuice and boil
vigorously. Add the stock and
cook until reduced by half, then
beat in the remaining chilled butter
to finish the sauce. Less than a
minute before serving add the
grapes to the sauce.

Carve the breast and legs from
the frames and serve one each per
person. Pour over the sauce and
serve immediately.

SERVES 6

POACHED QUAIL OR PARTRIDGE

Wrap quail or partridge in vine leaves and poach slowly in 185 ml
verjuice and 4 tablespoons extra-virgin olive oil. Reconstitute sultanas,
raisins or currants in verjuice and add to the juices. If desired, warm
as little as 125 ml jellied chicken stock and add to the poaching pan
while the birds are resting to make a beautiful jus.

PARTRIDGE WITH SAVOY CABBAGE, PANCETTA, WALNUTS AND VERJUICE

Partridge with cabbage has to be the most traditional of combinations, and was the one I rejected for the longest. I'm now sorry I did: Savoy cabbage, properly cooked, provides the perfect foil to the richness and density of partridge breast, and the gentle acidity of the verjuice balances the sweetness of the cabbage.

If you don't have a really large casserole, it may be better to split the following ingredients between two dishes when cooking.

24 freshly shelled walnuts
4 partridge
1 lemon
sea salt
freshly ground black pepper
3 tablespoons duck fat *or* butter
1 large sprig rosemary
8 thin slices mild pancetta
1 Savoy cabbage
250 ml verjuice
unsalted butter

Preheat the oven to 220°C. Dry-roast the walnuts for 6–8 minutes, shaking the tray to prevent the nuts from burning. If the walnuts are not fresh season's, rub them in a clean tea towel to remove the bitter skins. Set aside.

Separate the legs from the breast of each partridge, keeping both legs attached and in one piece and the breast on the frame. Squeeze lemon juice into the cavity of each bird and season. Melt the duck fat with half the rosemary in a heavy-based enamelled casserole with a tight-fitting lid. Brown each partridge very slowly on all sides. Remove the partridge from the casserole and allow them to cool, then wrap 2 slices of pancetta over each breast. Set the casserole aside with the duck fat in it.

Wash, trim and shred the cabbage. Toss the cabbage in the residual duck fat in the casserole over medium heat, then season very well and pour in the verjuice. Put the partridge on top, then season again and cover with the lid. Increase the heat so that the verjuice reduces and the cabbage cooks in about 5 minutes. The breasts may be ready ahead of the legs. If the breasts feel firm, take them out and keep them warm, covered, while the legs finish cooking (they may only need another 5 minutes – check by piercing a leg at its thickest point to see if the juices run clear). While the legs are finishing cooking, bring a knob of butter to nut-brown with the remaining rosemary, then toss the walnuts in it and tip the lot into the cabbage, discarding the rosemary. Serve immediately.

SERVES 4

ROASTING POULTRY
Paint roasting poultry with verjuice, olive oil and fresh herbs to caramelise the skin wonderfully.

ROAST DUCK WITH
VERJUICE SAUCE

This recipe, from the excellent Melbourne restaurant Becco, first appeared in a collection put together by Garry Crittenden of Dromana Estate winery.

4 × 1.8 kg ducks
10 carrots
2 onions
4 sticks celery
water
1 teaspoon tomato paste
1 bouquet garni
1 leek
butter
4 small bunches Pinot Noir grapes
200 ml verjuice

Preheat the oven to 240°C.
Put the ducks into a large pot with 1 carrot, 1 onion and 1 stick of celery, all roughly chopped, and add water to just cover. Bring to a boil and simmer gently for 10 minutes. Remove the ducks and allow to drain. Discard the cooking liquid.

Halve 7 of the remaining carrots and arrange in a baking dish. Put the ducks on top and roast for about 30 minutes or until browned all over. Remove from the oven and discard the carrots.

When the ducks are cool enough to handle, cut each one in half and remove the thigh, wing and rib bones. Set the ducks aside and put the bones into a stockpot.

Add the tomato paste and bouquet garni to the stockpot and cover the bones with water. Roughly chop the leek and the remaining carrots, onion and celery and brown them in a little butter in a frying pan, then transfer to the stockpot. Bring the pot to a boil and simmer for about 4 hours, skimming when necessary.

Strain the stock and reduce over a high heat to a sauce-like consistency. Set aside.

Preheat the oven to 250°C. Reheat the halved ducks in a baking dish with a little of the stock. Meanwhile, fry the bunches of grapes in a little butter until golden, then deglaze the pan with the verjuice. Reduce this liquid by half, then add the duck stock and bring it to a boil. By this stage the ducks should be crispy.

To serve, put half a duck on each plate, then pour over the sauce and garnish with a bunch of grapes.

SERVES 8

WARM DUCK SALAD
Toss roast duck, baby spinach, walnuts, red onion and chopped, seeded pickled cumquats (see page 22) in a little extra-virgin olive oil over heat, then deglaze the pan with red-wine vinegar.

ROAST DUCK WITH LIVER AND WALNUT STUFFING

My family eats a lot of poultry – my elder daughter Saskia and her husband, Greg, run Barossa Farm Produce and are forever finding farmers to grow out birds slowly on antibiotic-free, vegetarian diets, and any 'seconds' inevitably come my way. We also have a great tradition of stuffing birds, and as a pretty competitive family there's always talk around the dinner table about who makes the best! The richness of this duck and its liver and walnut stuffing is beautifully offset by the clean flavour of the verjuice and grapes.

1 × 2.5–3 kg muscovy duck
extra-virgin olive oil
3 tablespoons verjuice
125 ml chicken stock
175 g small grapes (such as
    sultana grapes)
sea salt
freshly ground black pepper

LIVER AND WALNUT STUFFING
50 g freshly shelled walnuts
50 g smoked bacon, rind removed
100 g duck livers
50–70 g butter
½ head of garlic, peeled and chopped

1 large onion, chopped
100 g fresh breadcrumbs
1 tablespoon freshly chopped thyme
1 tablespoon freshly chopped
    rosemary
2 tablespoons freshly chopped
    flat-leaf parsley
sea salt
freshly ground black pepper

To make the stuffing, preheat the oven to 220°C. Dry-roast the walnuts on a baking tray in the oven for about 10 minutes, shaking the tray occasionally to prevent the nuts from burning. If the walnuts are not fresh season's, rub them in a clean tea towel while still hot to remove the bitter skins. Set aside.

Grill the bacon or fry it in a small non-stick frying pan until golden but not crisp, then dice it. Don't rinse out the pan. Cut the duck livers into quarters and remove any gall or sinew. Melt 25 g of the butter in the bacon pan, then add the liver and sear over medium heat until browned all over but still pink in the middle. Remove the liver from the pan and wipe the pan clean. Melt another 25 g of the butter in the pan, then add the garlic and onion and cook over medium heat for 5 minutes or until soft. Add the breadcrumbs and stir until golden, then add the herbs and walnuts and mix well, adding more butter if the mixture seems too dry. Season with salt and pepper.

Preheat the oven to 160°C. If the duck was vacuum-packed, blot it dry with paper towel, then fill the cavity with the stuffing. Put the duck into a large oven bag and tie

to secure. Transfer, breast-side down, to a baking dish greased with olive oil and roast for 2 hours or until the meat is tender.

Leaving the duck in the oven, increase the temperature to 220°C. When the oven has come up to temperature, remove the duck. Open the oven bag and tip the cooking juices into a small bowl, then discard the bag. Return the duck to the baking dish and roast for a further 10 minutes to crisp and brown the skin. Remove the duck from the baking dish and allow to rest, partially covered, in a warm place for 15 minutes. Meanwhile, refrigerate the bowl of cooking juices and skim away the fat that sets on top.

Stand the baking dish over medium heat, then add the skimmed cooking juices, verjuice and chicken stock and bring to a boil, stirring. Warm the grapes through in the sauce for 1–2 minutes, then season. Carve the duck and serve with the stuffing and grape sauce.

SERVES 4

SALAD OF DUCK LIVER, GREEN APPLE, WALNUTS AND CARAMELISED GARLIC

I recently found among my scribblings in a notebook from a trip to Paris a list of ingredients, with nothing more to identify what it was I had eaten and where I had eaten it. But reading the list immediately activated my memory – and my tastebuds. And so this composed salad came into being. Such salads are a moveable feast, able to change with the season. If the duck liver and verjuice are taken as a base, the apple could be replaced by fennel and shallots could be included instead of garlic. And so on and so on . . .

12 freshly shelled walnuts
12 cloves garlic
500 g duck livers
2 witlof bulbs
1 handful cress *or* rocket
2 Granny Smith apples
verjuice
unsalted butter
1 teaspoon fresh thyme leaves
sea salt
freshly ground black pepper
walnut oil
lemon juice

Preheat the oven to 200°C. Dry-roast the walnuts in the oven on a baking tray for about 10 minutes, shaking the tray occasionally to prevent the nuts from burning. If the walnuts are not fresh season's, rub them in a clean tea towel while still hot to remove the bitter skins.

Bring a small saucepan of water to a boil, then blanch the peeled garlic cloves for 5 minutes. Drain.

Trim the livers and discard any connective tissue. Separate the witlof leaves, then wash and spin-dry the cress or rocket. Peel and quarter the apples, then sprinkle with verjuice to prevent discolouring.

Melt a knob of butter in a frying pan and cook until nut-brown, then pan-fry the apple with the garlic cloves, thyme, salt and pepper until golden. Remove the apple and garlic to a plate. Add a little more butter to the pan, then season the livers and cook each side for about a minute. Add a splash of verjuice to the pan to deglaze it, and set aside to rest.

Make a vinaigrette of walnut oil, verjuice, a little lemon juice to taste, salt and pepper, then toss with the salad leaves, warm apple, livers, garlic cloves and walnuts and serve.

SERVES 4

ROASTING GAME BIRDS
Game birds are best roasted at a high temperature for a short time and then rested for a long time. Pour a little stock and verjuice over the resting bird for a delicious jus.

Meat

CHARGRILLED SCOTCH FILLET WITH SWEET POTATO

MARINATED LAMB

CARPACCIO OF LAMB WITH CUMQUATS AND GREEN PEPPERCORNS

ROAST LEG OF PORK WITH VERJUICE

FILLET OF PORK WITH SAGE AND VERJUICE

GLAZED LEG OF HAM

SASKIA'S WALNUT, MUSHROOM AND PROSCIUTTO TART

BRAISED RABBIT WITH VERJUICE

RABBIT PIES

LITTLE RABBIT PUDDINGS

CHARGRILLED SCOTCH FILLET WITH VERJUICE SAUCE AND SWEET POTATO

This recipe, from the former Melbourne restaurant Marchetti's Latin, first appeared in a collection put together by Garry Crittenden of Dromana Estate winery.

10 shallots, finely sliced

olive oil

375 ml verjuice

1 litre beef stock

3 large sweet potatoes

20 g butter

50 ml cream

sea salt

freshly ground black pepper

3 large potatoes

6 × 250 g yearling Scotch fillet steaks

In a saucepan, sauté the shallots in a little olive oil until golden, then deglaze the pan with the verjuice and reduce by half. Add the beef stock and bring to a boil. Simmer until the sauce has reduced and is sticky, then set aside.

Preheat the oven to 180°C. Roast the sweet potatoes in their skins until soft (about 45 minutes), then remove from the oven and allow to cool. Peel the sweet potatoes when cold and purée the flesh. Add the butter and cream and season to taste.

Peel the potatoes, then slice finely and pat dry with kitchen paper. Heat a good quantity of oil in a deep-sided pot and lower a few slices of potato into the oil when it is very hot. Cook until golden and transfer to crumpled kitchen paper to drain. Season, then keep warm while cooking the remaining chips.

Chargrill the steaks until rare to medium–rare, then remove from the grill and rest for 5–10 minutes. Meanwhile, warm the sweet potato purée and the sauce separately. Return the steaks to the chargrill and cook until medium–rare. Put a steak on each warmed plate, then top with some mashed sweet potato and add a potato chip. Top this with another layer of mash, then another chip, to make a tower on top of the steak. Pour the sauce around the steak and serve immediately.

SERVES 6

PAN-FRIED PORK WITH RHUBARB
Pork pan-fried with rhubarb or sorrel and then deglazed with verjuice is almost 'sour on sour' but works particularly well, especially with fatty meat.

MARINATED LAMB

I like to use milk-fed lamb or veal for this recipe, as it is so tender and flavoursome, and I like to serve the meat with red capsicum and red onion grilled on the barbecue and tossed with olives, extra-virgin olive oil and flat-leaf parsley.

Ask your butcher to bone the leg of lamb into a rectangular shape, as regular in thickness as possible. For the best results, you need a barbecue with a grill and a hotplate, but it's possible to use a kettle barbecue, too, if you're careful.

1 × 1.5 kg boned leg of lamb
2 cloves garlic, sliced
3 tablespoons extra-virgin olive oil
leaves from 2 sprigs rosemary
sea salt
freshly ground black pepper
a generous dash of verjuice
4 bay leaves

RESTING MARINADE
2 preserved lemon quarters
4 tablespoons extra-virgin olive oil
3 tablespoons verjuice
3 shallots, finely sliced
¼ cup freshly chopped flat-leaf
   parsley
freshly ground black pepper

Make incisions in the fat of the lamb and insert pieces of the garlic. Combine the olive oil, rosemary, salt and pepper and rub thoroughly into the lamb. Sprinkle the meat with verjuice and dot with bay leaves, then leave to marinate for several hours.

When you are ready to cook the meat, preheat the barbecue to hot. To make the resting marinade, discard the pulp from the preserved lemon and dice the rind, then mix with the remaining ingredients. Pour the marinade into a dish large enough to hold the lamb and set aside.

Seal the meat on the hot grill, skin-side down, until it caramelises. Depending on the heat of the grill, this may take a good 5 minutes. Reduce the heat to medium and seal the other side on the solid plate of the barbecue for 5 minutes. Continue this process of turning the meat until it is cooked, being careful not to burn it (this will take 20–30 minutes, depending on the age of the lamb and how pink you like your meat).

If the meat is cooking too fast, wrap it in foil after you have sealed both sides and continue as above (you can even finish it off in the oven, if you like).

When the meat is cooked, slip it gently into the resting marinade (having removed the foil, if you've used it). Rest for a good 15 minutes, turning once during this time. The marinade will combine deliciously with the meat juices.

SERVES 4

BARBECUED VEAL
Moisten tender young veal with olive oil and grill it very quickly on the barbecue. Drizzle the resting meat with verjuice.

CARPACCIO OF LAMB WITH CUMQUATS, GREEN PEPPERCORNS AND VERJUICE

I've written about Noel and Ian Tolley and their Riverland citrus orchards a number of times. Noel cleverly value-adds her entire cumquat crop by producing glacé whole cumquats and dried cumquat slices, both of which I love using. But I also love using the fresh fruit and am continually trying to find other farmers willing to plant cumquats commercially.

1 teaspoon green peppercorns
¼ cup dried cumquat slices
verjuice
1 × 300 g fillet of lamb
extra-virgin olive oil
squeeze of lemon juice
2 tablespoons freshly plucked
    coriander leaves

In separate bowls, soak the green peppercorns and dried cumquat slices in verjuice overnight, covered.

Next day, trim the meat of all sinew, then brush it with a little olive oil to minimise oxidation and wrap firmly in plastic film to form a log. To aid slicing, freeze the meat for about 20 minutes until it has firmed up. Using a very sharp knife, slice the meat finely. Arrange the pieces of meat on a sheet of plastic film, leaving space between each one, then cover with another sheet of plastic. Using a wooden mallet or rolling pin, gently flatten or roll the meat until each slice is paper-thin. Arrange the meat on 4 plates, allowing each slice to touch the next.

Combine 4 tablespoons extra-virgin olive oil with 1 tablespoon verjuice and the lemon juice to make a vinaigrette, then toss in the reconstituted cumquats and green peppercorns and the coriander leaves. Drizzle the dressing over the lamb and serve immediately.

SERVES 4

LAVENDER-MARINATED LAMB
Marinate boned legs of lamb ready for barbecuing in individual serves in verjuice, diced preserved lemon, lavender, dill and garlic. Serve with labne.

ROAST LEG OF PORK
WITH VERJUICE

In this rich, verjuice-flavoured twist on an old favourite, it is important that the basting liquid doesn't evaporate during the roasting process. The basting juices should caramelise the fennel and garlic in the bottom of the baking dish, while keeping the meat moist at the same time.

1 teaspoon fennel seeds

150 ml verjuice

250 ml chicken stock

6 fennel bulbs

24 cloves garlic, unpeeled

4 bay leaves

1 sprig thyme

freshly ground black pepper

3 teaspoons sea salt

1 × 2 kg leg of pork, rind scored

water

extra-virgin olive oil

Preheat the oven to 210°C. Toss the fennel seeds over heat in a dry frying pan until fragrant, then allow to cool a little before grinding with a mortar and pestle. Set aside. Mix the verjuice and chicken stock in a bowl, then set this aside too.

Trim the fennel bulbs and cut them in half lengthwise. Put the fennel into a baking dish and scatter with the garlic cloves, bay leaves and thyme, then season with pepper. Mix the sea salt with the ground fennel seeds and rub thoroughly into the pork, then put the meat on top of the vegetables, skin-side up. Pour in enough water to just cover the base of the baking dish, then roast for 30 minutes.

Reduce the oven temperature to 175°C and roast the meat for another 1½ hours, basting every 20 minutes with the verjuice and stock mixture. Keep an eye on the juices in the pan as the verjuice can cause burning – if necessary, add a little water or some of the verjuice and stock mixture, if you still have it. Pierce the thickest part of the meat with a skewer: if the juices run clear, the meat is cooked. Remove from the oven.

Transfer the vegetables to a serving platter and keep warm. Add any remaining verjuice and stock mixture to the hot baking dish, then cover and leave the meat to rest for 20 minutes to let the juices mingle. Serve with boiled waxy potatoes and a peppery rocket salad.

SERVES 6

VERJUICE AND QUINCE PASTE GLAZE
Make a glaze for chops or a rack of lamb (fat left on) by gently melting a little quince paste thinned down with some verjuice. Brush the glaze generously over the meat, then roll the chops or rack in freshly chopped rosemary and season with sea salt before barbecuing.

FILLET OF PORK WITH
SAGE AND VERJUICE

This is almost too easy, and a different example of how to deglaze with verjuice.

2 × 400 g fillets of pork

30 ml extra-virgin olive oil

2 cloves garlic, minced

sea salt

freshly ground black pepper

32 sage leaves

110 ml verjuice

60 g butter

Preheat the oven to 190°C. Trim the meat, then mix the olive oil, garlic, salt and pepper and brush the meat with it. Press a few of the sage leaves onto the meat, then seal the pork well on all sides over gentle heat in a heavy-based baking dish that takes the meat snugly. Deglaze the pan with the verjuice, then roast the meat for 15 minutes. Remove the meat from the oven and allow to rest, covered, for 10 minutes. Increase the oven temperature to 200°C.

Dot the remaining sage leaves with the butter and crisp them in the oven for 9 minutes, then tip them over the resting meat. Carve the pork and serve it with creamy mashed potato.

SERVES 4

My friend Damien Pignolet, of Sydney's Bistro Moncur, is a great chef and a teacher extraordinaire. His delivery is absolutely meticulous and yet he has the generosity of spirit to enjoy cooking with a disorganised person like me!

I love the sweetness of verjuice, particularly in spring when it is fresh. I use it principally in vinaigrettes and beurre blanc and to refresh sauces. I also use it in a court-bouillon when preparing brains, and prefer it to the more usual vinegar in agrodolce, a versatile Italian sweet–sour sauce that can be used with poultry, hare and vegetables. [I particularly like agrodolce with zucchini – see page 39. *Maggie*.]

I cook Marcella Hazan's dish of lamb with beans and vinegar from her *Second Classic Italian Cooking* with verjuice rather than vinegar. Here, onion is cooked in a generous amount of olive oil until golden brown, then diced shoulder is added and sealed well. The meat is covered with verjuice and boiled for 30 seconds. Beans, stalk-ends removed, are added to the pot, which is then covered with greaseproof paper. Check the seasoning and cook at 120°C for 1½ hours.

DAMIEN PIGNOLET

GLAZED LEG OF HAM

There is a world of difference between traditionally made and smoke-injected hams – having easy access to sugar-cured Barossa hams has spoiled me. It's worth pursuing a network of specialist suppliers.

Traditionally, cloves are often dotted over the glazed surface of a ham, but I find their flavour too strong and instead use dried figs. These almost burn in the cooking, which gives their sweetness a slightly bitter edge. Using verjuice instead of the more conventional wine ensures a really good caramelised glaze, and nothing is more attractive (to me at least) than the slightly singed pieces of fat. In our house it's always a race to see who cuts off those bits first!

1 × 7 kg leg of ham
175 g brown sugar
125 ml Dijon mustard
375 ml verjuice
400 g dried figs

Preheat the oven to 220°C. Strip the leathery skin from the ham. I find there is usually no need to remove any fat from under the skin – a covering of 5 mm–1 cm is what you are after. Place the ham in a baking dish.

Mix the sugar and mustard to a paste and pat it evenly over the top and sides of the ham. Score the fat quite deeply into a diamond pattern but be careful not to cut through to the meat.

Pour half the verjuice into the base of the baking dish and bake the ham for 15 minutes for the glaze to adhere. Reduce the oven temperature to 200°C.

Cut the figs in half and carefully fix them into the corners of the diamonds with toothpicks. Pour the remaining verjuice over the ham without dislodging the glaze. Add a little water to the baking dish to prevent the juices from burning, if necessary. (The verjuice will allow some glazing on the underside of the ham.) Bake the ham for another 10 minutes, then allow it to cool before serving.

PAN-FRIED SWEETBREADS
Poach and press sweetbreads overnight. Next day, pan-fry the sliced sweetbreads in nut-brown butter and deglaze the pan with verjuice. Exceptional!

SASKIA'S WALNUT, MUSHROOM
AND PROSCIUTTO TART

Long ago I had a book, now lost and its title forgotten, that included a recipe with many of the following ingredients. At the time I wrote the ingredients on a card, added the verjuice and changed the pastry. One day, my daughter Saskia picked up the card and changed the whole concept by the way in which she put the tart together. The result was such a success that the tart has been known ever since as 'Saskia's'.

100 g dried boletus mushrooms

3 tablespoons verjuice

400 g freshly shelled walnuts

2 slices white bread with crusts on
(about 75 g)

125 ml milk

10–12 slices prosciutto

2 cloves garlic

1 kg button mushrooms

butter

sea salt

freshly ground black pepper

SOUR CREAM PASTRY

300 g chilled unsalted butter

375 g plain flour

185 ml sour cream

To make the pastry, chop the chilled butter into small pieces and place it with the flour in a food processor. Pulse until the mixture resembles breadcrumbs. Add the sour cream and pulse again until the dough has just incorporated into a ball. Wrap carefully in plastic film and chill for 20 minutes. Roll out the pastry and line a 20 cm loose-bottomed flan tin. Chill for 20 minutes.

Reconstitute the dried boletus mushrooms in the verjuice for 30 minutes. Meanwhile, preheat the oven to 200°C.

Line the pastry case with foil, then fill it with dried beans and blind bake for 15 minutes. Remove the foil and beans and return the pastry case to the oven for a further 5 minutes. Remove from the oven and reset to 220°C.

Roast the walnuts on a baking tray for about 5 minutes, shaking the tray to prevent the nuts from burning. If the walnuts are not fresh season's, rub them in a clean tea towel to remove the bitter skins.

Toast the bread in the oven until golden, then cut it into cubes and soak in the milk until softened, then squeeze out the milk. Slice the prosciutto finely and chop the garlic. Blend the soaked toast, prosciutto, garlic and walnuts in a food processor to make a paste, then set aside.

Chop the button mushrooms and sauté them in a little butter over quite a high heat (do them in batches so they don't stew), then season well. Toss the reconstituted boletus mushrooms in a little more melted butter, then season and purée in a food processor.

To assemble the tart, spread the walnut and prosciutto paste over the base, then brush with the boletus purée and arrange the sautéd mushrooms on top. Bake for about 20 minutes until the edge of the pastry case is golden brown. Serve warm or at room temperature.

SERVES 8

BRAISED RABBIT
WITH VERJUICE

This recipe, from Tracey Lister when she was at the wonderful old Kingston Hotel in the inner-Melbourne suburb of Richmond, first appeared in a collection put together by Garry Crittenden of Dromana Estate winery.

2 wild *or* farmed rabbits
salt
freshly ground black pepper
olive oil
2 onions
2 cloves garlic
200 g kaiserfleisch
700 ml chicken stock
1 teaspoon capers
6 anchovy fillets

MARINADE
500 ml verjuice
8 sprigs thyme
1 bay leaf
6 cloves garlic

Cut the rabbits into 6 pieces. Put all the marinade ingredients into an enamelled or stainless steel pot and marinate the rabbit overnight.

Next day, preheat the oven to 160°C. Remove the rabbit from the marinade (reserve the marinade) and pat it dry with kitchen paper. Season. Heat a little olive oil in a large frying pan and seal the rabbit on all sides. Dice the onions, garlic and kaiserfleisch, then add this to the pan with the rabbit and cook until softened. Transfer the rabbit and flavourings to a large baking dish.

Deglaze the frying pan with the marinade and reduce by one-third. Add the chicken stock and bring to a boil, then pour over the rabbit. Cover the baking dish with foil and bake for 1½–2 hours.

To serve, grind the capers and anchovies to a paste in a mortar and pestle. Transfer the rabbit to a warm serving dish, then reduce the cooking liquid to a sauce consistency and stir in the anchovy paste. Pour the sauce over the rabbit and serve immediately with your favourite winter vegetables.

SERVES 4–6

RABBIT WITH ONIONS, PANCETTA AND ROSEMARY

Seal rabbit legs gently in a heavy-based pot with tiny onions, pancetta and rosemary or thyme and add a mixture of chicken stock and verjuice, then cover the pot tightly and simmer at a very low temperature until the meat falls from the bone. Toss in prunes towards the end, if you like. Perfect served with a grainy mustard.

RABBIT PIES

I have also used a confit of rabbit legs for this pie, picking the meat free of any bones and sinew. The recipe would work equally well for chicken that has been cooked, taken from the bone and cubed. The only recooking that is required is the baking of the pie pastry.

60 g pitted prunes

verjuice

1 farmed rabbit

extra-virgin olive oil

fresh thyme

sea salt

freshly ground black pepper

200 ml veal stock

200 ml rabbit *or* chicken stock

1½ quantities Sour Cream Pastry
(see pages 118–19)

50 g roasted flaked almonds

2 sprigs oregano, chopped

1 egg yolk

dash of cream

Put the prunes into a bowl and steep in verjuice overnight. Next day, drain and chop the prunes.

Preheat the oven to 180°C. Joint the rabbit by cutting the front and back legs away, leaving the saddle in one piece. Smother the rabbit with olive oil and rub with thyme, salt and pepper. Roast until the flesh is set, 15–20 minutes for the saddle and a little longer for the legs. Allow to rest, then carve the meat off the bone.

When cool, cut the meat into neat, even chunks, discarding any sinew as you go – you need 500 g cooked meat for the filling. Set aside.

Reduce 400 ml verjuice over heat until 100 ml remains. Allow to cool completely.

In separate saucepans, reduce the veal and rabbit or chicken stocks by half, then allow to cool.

Make and chill the pastry as instructed. Roll out the chilled pastry and line 6 × 125 ml moulds, leaving a 2 cm 'lip'. Roll out the remaining pastry and cut round lids slightly larger than the moulds. Refrigerate the lined moulds and lids for 20 minutes.

Combine the cold verjuice and stock reductions with the meat, almonds and oregano. Divide the filling between the lined moulds, then position the lids and press the edges together to ensure a good seal. Refrigerate the pies until required.

Preheat the oven to 150°C. Mix the egg yolk with a little cream and brush over the pastry. Bake for 8 minutes, then reduce the heat to 130°C and bake until golden brown and crispy. The pies should come out of their moulds easily and the bottoms should be golden. The time it takes for the pastry to cook is enough to ensure the pie is heated right through without overcooking the filling.

MAKES 6

WILD RABBIT
You can use wild rabbit to make these pies, too. However, you'll need two rabbits rather than one, and you'll have to poach rather than roast them to ensure they're not too dry. The jointed rabbit is poached gently in chicken stock with fresh thyme, garlic and a bay leaf – it must cook at a very low temperature, making a crockpot or pressure cooker a good option here.

LITTLE RABBIT PUDDINGS

I first made this dish for my winemaking friend Peter Lehmann when he was launching his Mentor series at Sydney's Regent Hotel and Melbourne's Grand Hyatt. I used partridge on the night but as it is hard to come by and as rabbit and verjuice have such an affinity, I've since cooked it as follows.

1 tablespoon sultanas

verjuice

2 farmed rabbits

3 tablespoons walnut oil

2 sprigs thyme

freshly ground black pepper

1 carrot, chopped

1 stick celery, chopped

extra-virgin olive oil

3 tablespoons white wine

water

butter

4 rashers very thinly cut
    streaky bacon

Soak the sultanas overnight in enough verjuice to just cover them. Next day, preheat the oven to 220°C. Remove the fillets from the rabbits, taking care to extract the liver and kidneys. Separate the silvery sinew on the rabbit fillets with a sharp knife and gently flatten each fillet between sheets of greaseproof paper with a wooden mallet until even. Mix 2 tablespoons verjuice with the walnut oil, thyme and some pepper, then marinate the fillets in this.

Remove the back legs and set aside for another use. Chop the remaining bones into quite small pieces with a cleaver. Toss the carrot and celery with a little olive oil and roast them with the chopped bones until caramelised, 30–40 minutes.

Deglaze the baking dish with the wine and tip the contents into a saucepan. Barely cover the vegetables and bones with water, then simmer for 2 hours to make a flavoursome stock. Remove the pot from the stove, then strain and chill. Remove any fat from the cold stock. Heat 250 ml of the stock with 125 ml verjuice in a clean saucepan and reduce by two-thirds over moderate heat, then remove from the heat. As it cools, the stock will become quite jellied.

If the kidneys and liver were available, pan-fry these until sealed but still retaining pinkness. Allow to cool.

Preheat the oven to 180°C. Smear the base and sides of 4 small ceramic soufflé dishes or dariole moulds with butter and then line them with some of the bacon, reserving enough to cover the dishes later. Layer the marinated meat, pan-fried kidneys and liver, sultanas and jellied stock in the moulds, then top with the remaining bacon and cover with baking paper.

Stand the moulds in a baking dish and pour in hot water to come two-thirds of the way up their sides. Bake for 20 minutes, then remove the baking dish from the oven and the moulds from the water. Allow the moulds to cool a little before gently inverting onto serving plates. Heat the leftover jellied stock and spoon it over the warm puddings before serving with lamb's lettuce or another delicate green salad dressed with a walnut oil and verjuice vinaigrette.

SERVES 6

Desserts

VERJUICE SORBET

FIGS STEWED IN AMARO SYRUP

CHOCOLATE CRESPELLE WITH MASCARPONE, FIGS AND STREGA

QUINCES AND PEARS POACHED IN VERJUICE

DRIED PEARS IN VERJUICE ON FILO WITH MASCARPONE

PEACHES STUFFED WITH AMARETTI, ALMONDS AND GINGER

CHESTNUT CAKE

APPLE TEA CAKE WITH CARAMELISED VERJUICE SYRUP

YOGHURT AND POLENTA CAKE WITH PEARS IN VERJUICE

CHRISTMAS PUDDING

VERJUICE SORBET

The heavy sugar syrup required for this sorbet is made by simply heating 1 part sugar to 1 part water, stirring, until the sugar has dissolved. The syrup is allowed to cool before being used. This recipe, from the original Mietta's at Queenscliff, Victoria, first appeared in a collection put together by Garry Crittenden of Dromana Estate winery.

2 litres verjuice

200 ml lemon juice

2.2 litres heavy sugar syrup

3 egg whites

Combine the verjuice, lemon juice and sugar syrup. Whisk the egg whites to a soft snow and fold into the liquid. Churn the mixture in an ice-cream machine according to the manufacturer's instructions.

MAKES 6 LITRES

VERJUICE SOUR

For a refreshing alcoholic cocktail, try this recipe, from the late Mietta O'Donnell at Mietta's at the Queenscliff Hotel. Shake together 120 ml verjuice, 30 ml Bacardi, 2 teaspoons lemon juice, 2 teaspoons Cointreau and some ice, then strain and serve immediately.

FIGS STEWED IN AMARO SYRUP

Summer produces two of my favourite ingredients: figs and verjuice. Seasonal marriages are always the best, and this one is taken to even greater heights by the addition of Amaro, a herbal digestive that originates in Italy's Abruzzo region. A honey semifreddo is a wonderful accompaniment, the warmth of the honey adding extra dimension. Stephanie Alexander created this recipe when we were in Tuscany for our cooking schools.

1 cup sugar

375 ml verjuice

½ vanilla bean, split

12 large figs, peeled

100 ml Amaro

3 tablespoons thick cream *or*
    mascarpone (optional)

Put the sugar, verjuice and vanilla bean into a large saucepan and heat gently until the sugar has dissolved. Add the figs and simmer gently, covered, for 5 minutes until tender, then let the figs cool in the syrup. Add the Amaro and leave for 30 minutes. Serve the figs and their juices on a flattish plate drizzled with cream or mascarpone.

SERVES 6

CHOCOLATE CRESPELLE WITH MASCARPONE, FIGS AND STREGA

This dessert or afternoon-tea treat is based on a recipe from a friend, chef James Fien. It became a great favourite during the cooking schools Stephanie Alexander and I held in Tuscany. Our friend Peter Lortz also made it once during those glorious few weeks by cooking the figs in the delicious Tuscan dessert wine vin santo instead of sprinkling them with Strega.

10 g butter

75 ml milk

4 eggs

2 teaspoons Strega

140 g plain flour

60 g Dutch cocoa

25 g sugar

1 teaspoon salt

icing sugar

FILLING

100 g dried figs

verjuice

2 teaspoons Strega

200 g mascarpone

Melt the butter in a saucepan over a gentle heat and allow it to turn nut-brown without burning, then cool a little. Mix the melted butter, milk, eggs and Strega in a bowl. Sift the dry ingredients, except the icing sugar, then whisk these into the butter mixture to make a batter. Rest the batter for 1 hour before cooking.

While the batter is resting, start the filling. Reconstitute the figs in verjuice – this will take about 20 minutes. Drain the figs extremely well, then chop them and sprinkle them with the Strega.

Pass the batter through a fine-meshed sieve into a jug. Heat a crêpe pan, then wipe it with a piece of buttered paper. Remove the pan from the heat and pour in a little batter, swirling it to spread the batter to the edges of the pan. Stand the pan over the heat again. After a minute, lift the thin outer edge of the crêpe with a fine spatula and flip to cook the other side. Remove the crêpe to a plate. Repeat this process with the remaining batter. Allow the crêpes to cool, then trim them to even them up.

Mix the figs carefully into the mascarpone. Do not overmix as the mascarpone will split. Pipe or spoon some of the filling onto the centre of each crêpe. Fold in the ends, then roll up the crêpes. Chill slightly before serving dusted with icing sugar.

MAKES 8

POACHED FRUIT
Poach fresh fruit – particularly peaches, quinces, nectarines or pears – in verjuice.

Sophie Zalokar, Barossa born and bred, was my apprentice for four years in the early days of the Pheasant Farm, and also helped me with the photo shoots for Maggie's Table. *She is a truly natural cook – in fact, we call her the bread witch as she has such an innate ability (her grandmother had also been called this years beforehand!). Cooking isn't Sophie's only talent: she also used to play the piano on Saturday nights when the main courses were done, went on to do fine arts at university, and in 2002 had her first book,* PicNic, *published to great acclaim.*

If I have verjuice on hand when our neighbour spoils us with fresh crays, I make a hollandaise with a reduction of verjuice as opposed to the usual wine and vinegar one. Delicious! Verjuice mixed with soda water and crushed ice is also a gift on a hot day.

But I must admit it is the sweet dishes that capture my imagination when using verjuice. I would like to experiment with an old-fashioned syllabub served with crisp almond bread, or even a charlotte in which the fruit, most likely apples, has been baked with verjuice and honey. I find verjuice has a particularly wonderful affinity with apples and almonds. I've also made a green grape and frangipane tart by tossing sultana grapes with a little sugar in foaming butter, then deglazing the pan with verjuice and reducing it until thick and syrupy. This is then spooned into a pastry case, topped with frangipane cream and baked until golden.

SOPHIE ZALOKAR

QUINCES AND PEARS
POACHED IN VERJUICE

Not having a particularly sweet tooth, I prefer using a verjuice syrup when cooking fruit as it gives a fresher edge than a sugar syrup would. As verjuice is a mild acidulant, it lifts flavours but doesn't mask them – if anything, the 'fruitiness' is enhanced.

3 quinces
juice of 1 lemon
1 kg beurre bosc pears
750 ml verjuice
sugar (optional)

Peel and core the quinces, then cut them into 8 slices and put them into water with the lemon juice to stop the fruit discolouring. Peel, core and quarter the pears. Poach the fruit in the verjuice with sugar to taste for 30–60 minutes in a large, flat baking dish or a saucepan. (The cooking time will depend on the variety and ripeness of the fruit.) The fruit should be soft to the touch but still intact and will not be the deep ruby-red of long-cooked quince.

Increase the heat and reduce the verjuice until both the fruit and verjuice caramelise – turn the slices of fruit once the first side has caramelised.

Serve with fresh cream, on a matchstick of puff pastry or with a delicate Italian lemon biscuit.

SERVES 6

DRIED PEARS IN VERJUICE ON
FILO WITH MASCARPONE

This dessert is just as delicious when made using dried plums, peaches or nectarines, all of which marry beautifully with verjuice.

250 ml verjuice
1 teaspoon castor sugar
500 g dried pears
15 sheets filo pastry
melted unsalted butter
250 ml mascarpone

Put the verjuice and sugar into a large, flat, non-reactive baking dish or saucepan and cook gently until the sugar has dissolved. Reduce the heat slightly and add the dried pears. Simmer slowly until the pears are soft to the touch but still intact. Remove the fruit from the pan and set aside. Increase the heat and reduce the liquid to a thick syrup. Allow to cool.

Preheat the oven to 220°C. Cut the filo pastry into rounds about 10 cm in diameter (you will get 2 rounds per sheet). Put the pastry rounds onto a baking tray lined with baking paper, brushing each piece of pastry with melted butter as you go. Your aim is to make 6 stacks, each with 5 layers. Bake the filo stacks for only a minute until they are golden brown and crisp. Remove from the oven. Arrange 3 pears on each filo stack, fanning them out to cover the pastry. Add a generous dollop of mascarpone, then drizzle a little syrup around and serve immediately.

SERVES 6

PEACHES STUFFED WITH AMARETTI, ALMONDS AND GINGER AND BAKED IN VERJUICE

Bitter almonds aren't easy to find – visit a nut-grower, if you can, and store the nuts in the freezer, where they'll stay fresh longer. Poisonous in large quantities, bitter almonds added in tiny amounts provide a unique dimension, as any marzipan-lover can attest.

The verjuice in which these peaches are cooked becomes a wonderful syrup during cooking as the buttery, sugary juices mingle.

½ cup unblanched almonds (including
   3 bitter almonds)
6 yellow peaches
80 g amaretti biscuits, crumbled
2 teaspoons brandy
1 teaspoon finely chopped
   glacé ginger
unsalted butter
125 ml verjuice

Preheat the oven to 180°C. Toast the almonds on a baking tray for 5–10 minutes, shaking the tray regularly to prevent the nuts from burning. Set the nuts aside to cool, then grind them in a food processor.

Halve and stone the peaches, then gouge out a little flesh and chop it. Combine the chopped fruit with the ground nuts, amaretti crumbs, brandy, glacé ginger and 60 g butter and pile the mixture into the cavities in the peach halves. Generously butter an ovenproof dish just large enough to hold the fruit neatly. Arrange the fruit in the dish and pour in the verjuice. Bake for 30 minutes until the fruit is tender but still holding its shape. Serve hot, warm or cold with the syrupy verjuice spooned around.

SERVES 6

CHESTNUT CAKE

This flat, dense cake is served in Italy with coffee. As much as I love chestnuts, they can be heavy and dense, even as flour. Here verjuice gives the palate a lift, while the chestnut flavour remains intact. Given that it is made from grapes, verjuice is the perfect medium for reconstituting currants, sultanas or raisins while adding another depth of flavour at the same time.

⅓ cup currants

verjuice

⅓ cup pine nuts

250 g chestnut flour

375 ml cold water

3 tablespoons extra-virgin olive oil

pinch of salt

1 sprig rosemary

grated zest of 1 orange

Strega (optional)

mascarpone (optional)

extra orange zest (optional)

Reconstitute the currants for about 30 minutes in enough verjuice to cover them.

Preheat the oven to 200°C. Dry-roast the pine nuts for about 10 minutes until golden brown (watch them carefully as they burn easily). Reduce the oven temperature to 190°C.

Sift the chestnut flour into a bowl, then stir in the cold water gradually to make a thick paste (you may not need it all). Make sure there are no lumps, then add the olive oil and salt.

Chop the rosemary and zest the orange, then add both to the batter with the drained currants and pine nuts and stir vigorously until amalgamated. Grease a shallow 20 cm cake tin and pour in the batter to a depth of 2.5 cm, then bake for 30 minutes.

Serve the cake warm, either moistened with Strega poured over it as soon as it comes out of the oven or with mascarpone flavoured with a little orange zest.

SERVES 8

LOQUATS IN VERJUICE SYRUP

Cut 500 g loquats into quarters and remove the stones (peel the fruit after cooking, if you like it peeled). Dissolve ½ cup castor sugar in 250 ml verjuice over a gentle heat, then simmer the loquats in this, with a little lemon zest if you like, for 10 minutes. Allow to cool, then remove the fruit and reduce the syrup a little more. The poached loquats are wonderful with a dollop of thick cream, and particularly good with a moist cake, such as the olive oil and Sauternes cake made famous by Chez Panisse.

APPLE TEA CAKE WITH
CARAMELISED VERJUICE SYRUP

Bathing a fresh apple tea cake in a caramel syrup made with verjuice makes a divine pudding. This recipe comes from Sophie Zalokar, one of my wonderful Pheasant Farm staff who is now very much part of our extended family. She has a natural flair with food (we love working out menus together – the tastebuds really work overtime!) and great organisational skills – she steps in from time to time even now to help me out with particularly big jobs, despite the fact that she now lives in Perth.

6 small golden delicious apples

castor sugar

250 ml verjuice

¾ teaspoon ground cassia

CAKE

100 g softened unsalted butter

100 g castor sugar

2 × 61 g eggs

250 g plain flour

1 teaspoon bicarbonate of soda

1 teaspoon cream of tartar

½ teaspoon salt

125 ml milk

1 teaspoon vanilla extract

CARAMELISED VERJUICE SYRUP

250 ml verjuice

240 g castor sugar

300 ml reserved apple cooking syrup

Peel and core the apples, then cut into eighths and put into a saucepan with 3 tablespoons castor sugar and verjuice. Bring to a boil over a high heat, then gently stir until the sugar has dissolved. Turn off the heat but don't move the pan. Leave the apple in this light syrup for 10 minutes, then drain, reserving the syrup (you should have about 300 ml).

Preheat the oven to 180°C and grease and line a 22 cm springform tin.

To make the cake, cream the butter and 3 tablespoons castor sugar until pale and thick. Add the eggs one at a time, beating well after each addition. (If the mixture starts to curdle, add a tablespoon of the measured flour to stabilise it.)

Sift the flour, bicarbonate of soda, cream of tartar and salt and add alternately to the egg mixture with the milk and vanilla extract. Spoon the batter into the prepared tin and smooth the top.

Arrange the apple over the cake in a concentric pattern, pushing the pieces into the batter slightly. Mix 2 teaspoons castor sugar and the ground cassia and sprinkle evenly over the top. Bake for 45 minutes or until a skewer inserted into the

centre of the cake comes out clean. Let the cake stand in the tin for at least 10 minutes, then remove the tin carefully.

While the cake is cooking, make the syrup. Have iced water ready in the sink or in a large bowl. Bring the verjuice and castor sugar to a boil in a saucepan and cook until a deep golden brown. Remove the caramel from the heat and cautiously add the reserved apple cooking syrup – the mixture may spit a little. Stand the saucepan in the iced water immediately to arrest the cooking, then pour into a jug ready to serve.

To serve, put a wedge of cake onto each plate (a plate with a gentle lip is best), then ladle over the syrup and offer with a hearty dollop of thick cream.

SERVES 8

YOGHURT AND POLENTA CAKE
WITH PEARS IN VERJUICE

This unusual, delicious dessert is from Philip Johnson of Brisbane's award-winning e'cco bistro.

6 firm pears, peeled and cored
250 ml plain Greek yoghurt
honey

CAKE
300 g plain yoghurt
100 g polenta
grated zest of 1 orange
grated zest of 1 lemon
125 g softened unsalted butter
220 g castor sugar
3 eggs
200 g self-raising flour
½ teaspoon bicarbonate of soda
80 g currants
80 g roasted pine nuts

VERJUICE SYRUP
500 ml verjuice
juice of 1 orange
juice of 1 lemon
1 stick cinnamon
1 vanilla bean, split
1 bay leaf

To make the cake, combine the yoghurt, polenta and zests and set aside for 1 hour. Meanwhile, preheat the oven to 180°C and grease and line a loaf tin.

Cream the butter and castor sugar until pale, then add the eggs one at a time, beating well after each addition. Sift the flour and bicarbonate of soda together and fold into the creamed mixture.

Fold in the yoghurt mixture, then stir in the currants and pine nuts.

Pour into the prepared tin and cook for about 45 minutes or until a skewer inserted into the cake comes out clean. Turn the cake out onto a wire rack to cool.

To make the verjuice syrup, bring all the ingredients to a boil in a stainless steel or enamelled saucepan. Reduce the heat and simmer over low heat for several minutes, then add the pears and

cook until tender. Let the pears cool completely in the syrup, then remove the cinnamon, vanilla bean and bay leaf. Leave the pears in the syrup until you are ready to use them.

To serve, put a slice of cake and a poached pear on each plate. Spoon a little syrup over and around the cake, then add a spoonful of Greek yoghurt alongside and drizzle with honey.

SERVES 6

TROPICAL FRUIT
Verjuice is perfect for preserving tropical fruit such as mangoes as the pH is low enough to extend shelf-life without masking flavour.

CHRISTMAS PUDDING

The cumquats in my plum pudding set it apart from other recipes; soaking them in verjuice makes even more of a difference. The pudding is so rich with fruit, but the verjuice adds a freshness, a piquancy.

Christmas puddings certainly mature with standing – I try to make ours in October – but the main issues are having the right balance of flavours in the first place and ensuring a long cooking time. Puddings can become mouldy if the weather is humid or if several are hung too close together, so if you don't have time to mature your pudding, or the weather is against you, it won't matter as long as the balance is fine.

115 g candied citron peel

250 g mixed peel

225 g currants

225 g seedless raisins

225 g sultanas

75 g flaked almonds

300 ml port

115 g plain flour

1 good pinch ground cinnamon

1 good pinch freshly grated nutmeg

1 good pinch ground ginger

1 good pinch ground mace

1 teaspoon salt

225 g chilled unsalted butter

225 g fresh breadcrumbs

3 free-range eggs

BRANDY BUTTER

175 g icing sugar

175 g softened unsalted butter

120 ml cumquat brandy *or*
160 ml brandy

Chop the citron peel, then combine it with the mixed peel, dried fruit, almonds and port in a large non-reactive bowl and mix thoroughly. Cover with plastic film and leave at room temperature for 24 hours, stirring several times.

Sift the flour, spices and salt into a large bowl, then grate in the butter coarsely. Stir in the breadcrumbs and add the fruit mixture. Whisk the eggs until light and frothy and stir through the pudding mixture until well combined.

Dust a 30 cm square of calico with a little flour, then spoon the mixture into the middle. Gather up the cloth and tie it securely with string at the top of the pudding. (You can also make 2 smaller puddings if you wish – just divide the mixture in half and wrap each separately.) Steam the pudding in a large double steamer or boil in a large saucepan for 6 hours, replenishing the water every 30 minutes or as necessary. Suspend the boiled pudding in a cool, airy place to mature before using.

Make the brandy butter on Christmas morning (it can be made the day before but needs to be wrapped really well to avoid it becoming tainted in the refrigerator). Cream the icing sugar and butter in an electric mixer until white, thick and fluffy and the sugar has dissolved. This takes some time, so be patient. Slowly beat in the brandy, a teaspoonful at a time, tasting as you go. Cover with plastic film and refrigerate.

To serve, steam the pudding in its cloth in the top of a steamer or double saucepan for 1 hour or until heated through. Meanwhile, let the brandy butter stand at room temperature for 20 minutes, then transfer it to 2 serving bowls.

This pudding makes wonderful eating cold, as a cake!

SERVES 16–20

DRIED FRUIT IN VERJUICE

Reconstitute dried fruit in verjuice, then poach the fruit in a sugar syrup balanced with verjuice. If the fruit has not been over-sulphured, make the sugar syrup with the soaking liquid and sugar alone.

BIBLIOGRAPHY

The following list of references includes those books I turned to for culinary inspiration and those that I used when researching the role verjuice has played throughout history.

Alexander, Stephanie and Beer, Maggie. *Stephanie Alexander & Maggie Beer's Tuscan Cookbook*. Viking, Ringwood, 1998.

Batmanglij, Najmieh. *The New Food of Life: A Book of Ancient Persian & Modern Iranian Cooking and Ceremonies*. Mage Publishers, Washington DC, 1992.

Beavilliers, A.B. *A Complete System of French Domestic Cookery: Formed upon Principles of Economy, and Adapted for the Use of Families of Moderate Fortune* (4th edition). S. Cornish, London, 1837.

Beer, Maggie. *Maggie's Farm*. Allen & Unwin, Sydney, 1993.

—— *Maggie's Orchard*. Viking, Ringwood, 1997.

—— *Maggie's Table*. Viking, Ringwood, 2001.

Boxer, Arabella. *Mediterranean Cookbook*. Penguin Books, Harmondsworth, 1981.

Bugialli, Giuliano. *The Fine Art of Italian Cooking*. Time Books, New York, 1979.

Castelvetro, Giacomo. *The Fruit, Herbs and Vegetables of Italy*. Viking Penguin, Harmondsworth, 1989.

David, Elizabeth. *French Provincial Cooking* (rev. edn). Penguin Books, Harmondsworth, 1970.

—— *Italian Food*. Penguin Books, Harmondsworth, 1989.

—— *An Omelette and a Glass of Wine*. J.M. Dent, Melbourne, 1984.

Davidson, Alan. *The Oxford Companion to Food*. Oxford University Press, Oxford, 1999.

Eaton, Mrs Mary. *The Cook and Housekeeper's Complete & Universal Dictionary* (new edn). W. Tegg, London, 1849.

Hammond, P.W. *Food and Feast in Medieval England*. Alan Sutton, England, 1993.

Henisch, Bridget Ann. *Fast and Feast: Food in Medieval Society*. Pennsylvania State University Press, University Park, 1976.

Kamman, Madeleine. *In Madeleine's Kitchen*. Atheneum, New York, 1984.

—— *When French Women Cook*. Atheneum, New York, 1982.

Kurlansky, Mark. *Cod: Biography of a Fish that Changed the World*. Vintage, Toronto, 1998.

Larousse Gastronomique. Paul Hamlyn, London, 1988.

Man, Rosamond and Weir, Robin. *The Compleat Mustard*. Constable and Company, London, 1988.

Petroni, Paolo and Maschietto, Deborah Hodges (trans.). *The Complete Book of Florentine Cooking*. Edizioni il Centauro SRL, Florence, 1995.

Pieri, Stefano de. *A Gondola on the Murray* (vol. 1). ABC Books, Sydney, 1999.

Roach, F.A. *Cultivated Fruits of Britain: Their Origin and History*. Basil Blackwell Inc., Oxford, 1985.

Root, Waverley. *Food: An Authoritative and Visual History and Dictionary of the Foods of the World*. Simon and Schuster, New York, 1980.

Santich, Barbara. *The Original Mediterranean Cuisine: Medieval Recipes for Today*. Wakefield Press, Adelaide, 1995.

Simeti, Mary Taylor. *Pomp and Sustenance*. Alfred A. Knopf, New York, 1989.

Soyer, A. *Pantropheon, or, History of Food, and Its Preparation, from the Earliest Ages of the World*. Simpkin, Marshall, London, 1853.

Spurling, Hilary. *Elinor Fettiplace's Receipt Book*. Penguin Books, Harmondsworth, 1987.

Tannahill, Reay. *Food in History*. Penguin Books, Harmondsworth, 1988.

Taruschio, Ann and Franco. *Leaves from the Walnut Tree*. Pavilion, London, 1993.

Toussaint-Samat, Maguelonne. *History of Food*. Blackwell Publishers, Oxford, 1994.

Willan, Anne. *Great Cooks and Their Recipes: From Taillevent to Escoffier*. Pavilion, London, 1995.

Wolfert, Paula. *The Cooking of South-West France*. The Dial Press, New York, 1983.

INDEX

MAGGIE'S TABLE

Maggie Beer is a long-time resident of South Australia's Barossa Valley. She is deeply involved in the food culture of the area as a producer, chef and enthusiastic champion of all the Valley has to offer.

Here are recipes and stories that capture the rich flavours and colours of Maggie's home. Season by season, we discover how she cooks with fresh, local produce for simple family dinners and large festive occasions. We travel with her to the local dairy for fresh cream to make ice-cream, to the butcher for smoked meats, and to the neighbouring beekeeper for delicious honey. The large wood oven in the garden is lit for baked lemony chicken and potatoes, a picnic is prepared to take to the local pine forest to search for mushrooms, and we join Maggie's husband, Colin, on a crabbing expedition in order to make classic crab cakes in the electric frypan.

Come sit at *Maggie's Table* to celebrate the art of country cooking and to share the generosity and *joie de vivre* of one of Australia's favourite cooks – the marvellous Maggie Beer.

ALSO BY MAGGIE BEER IN PENGUIN

STEPHANIE ALEXANDER & MAGGIE BEER'S TUSCAN COOKBOOK

In September 1997, Stephanie Alexander and Maggie Beer journeyed to Italy to run three cooking schools for Australian students. For two months they lived in the heart of Tuscany, in a beautiful villa nestled among the vineyards and fields to the south of Siena.

As two cooks and food lovers who respect any landscape in which they find themselves, Stephanie and Maggie immersed themselves in Tuscan culinary traditions. They found that Tuscan food is very seasonal – if it's not ripe, it's not available – and that the Tuscan style of cooking preserves that freshness of flavour. Central to the cuisine are olive oil, bread, tomatoes and wine, and grilling over a fire, which in Australia we might call barbecuing, is the preferred method. The fresh and delicious recipes in this book are based on those used in Stephanie and Maggie's cooking schools.

Breathtaking photography by Simon Griffiths captures the food, culture, architecture, countryside and people of the region, along with the talent and cooking ideas of these two much-loved Australian cooks.